# THE TOM WOLFE
# TREASURY OF PATTERNS

# 108

## Animal Patterns

### Tom Wolfe

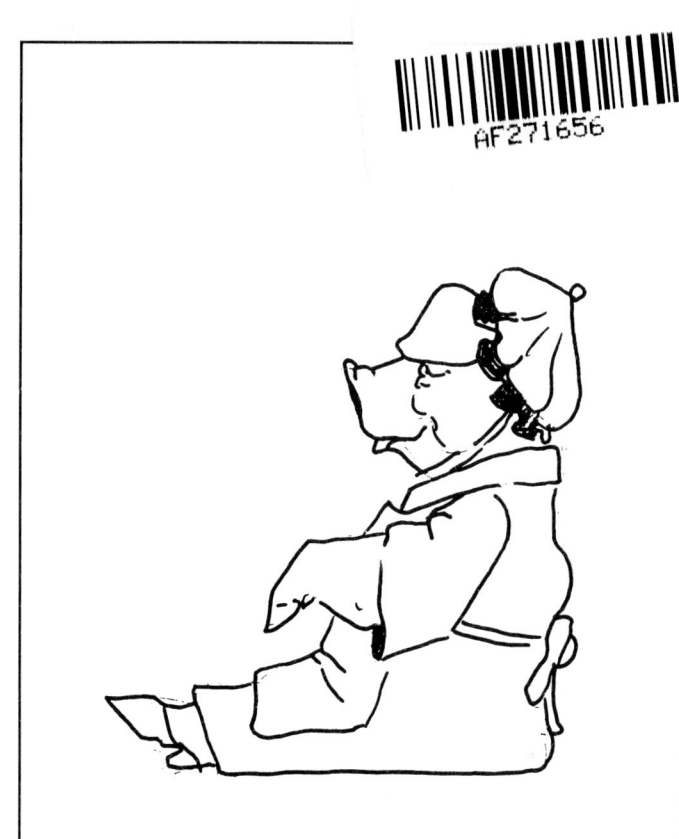

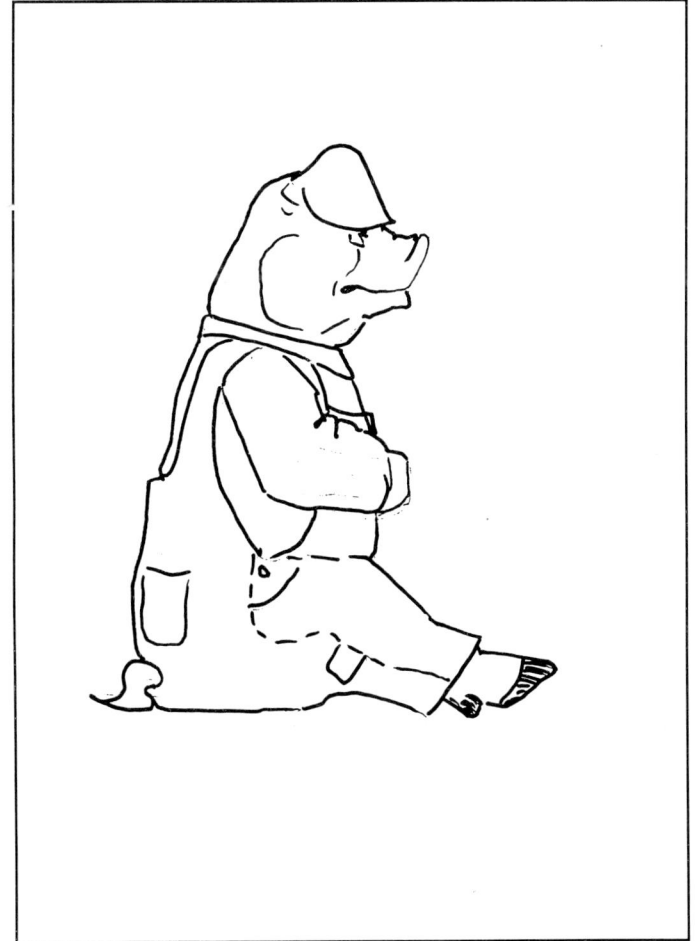

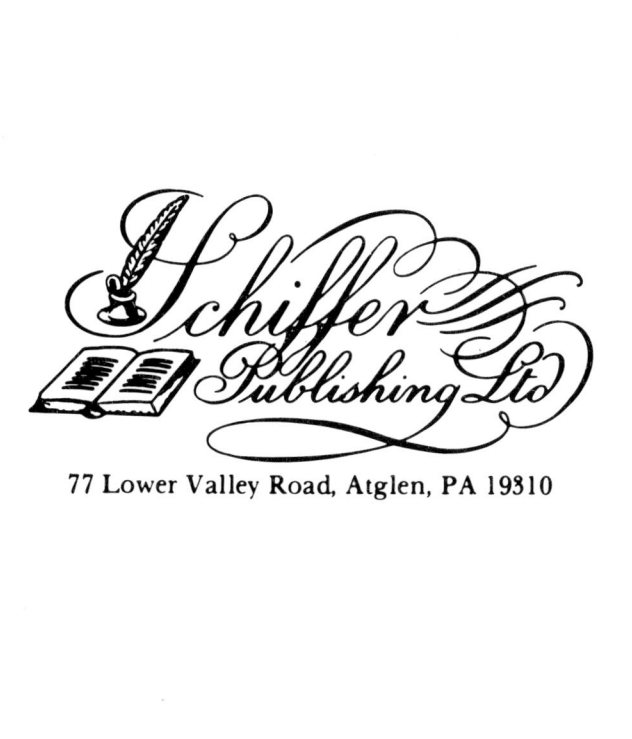

77 Lower Valley Road, Atglen, PA 19310

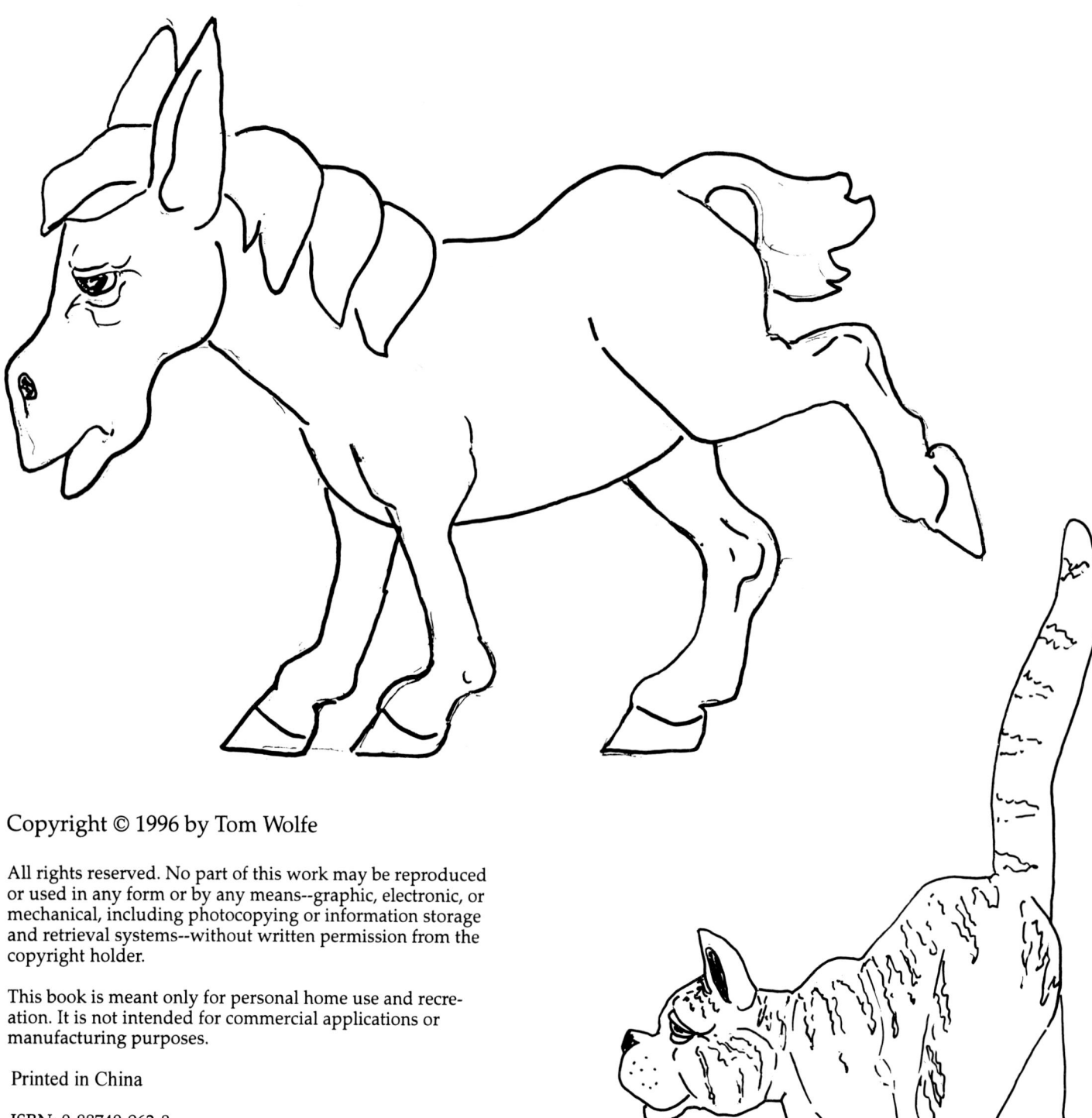

Printed in China

ISBN: 0-88740-962-8

**Library of Congress Cataloging-in-Publication Data**

Wolfe, Tom ( Tom James)
    The Tom Wolfe treasury of patterns:108 animal patterns/
Tom Wolfe.
        p.    cm.
    ISBN 0-88740-962-8  (paper)
    1. Wood-carving--Patterns. 2. Animals in art. I. Title.
TT199.7.W6437    1996
731'.832--dc20
                                            95-50883
                                            CIP

Published by Schiffer Publishing, Ltd.
77 Lower Valley Road
Atglen, PA 19310
Please write for a free catalog.
This book may be purchased from the publisher.
Please include $2.95 postage.
Try your bookstore first.

We are interested in hearing from authors
with book ideas on related subjects.

# Introduction

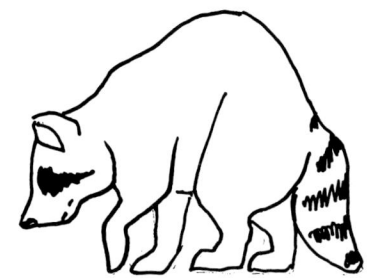

For nearly every carving I do, I create a new pattern. Even if the differences from an earlier work are only minor, I find it helpful to draw the changes on paper. There are a lot of reasons for this. Practically, it is easier to fix my mistakes on paper than it is in wood. But more importantly, I find it helps the creative process. The figures take on their personality in two-dimensions, before they come to life in three dimensions, and I like to see the effects before I carve a figure in the wood.

As you can imagine, after nearly forty years of carving, day after day, week after week, I've got a pretty deep pile of these patterns around my shop. Now some of them had a few spots of barbecue on them and some of them were a little beat up, but they were good enough for me to recopy and share with you.

As any of you who have read my other books know, it is my practice to only do a pattern in profile. I get a few angry letters about that now and then, accusing me of "keeping secrets." The truth is that even in my own carving I do it this way.

I do it for a couple of reasons. First, I find that if you try to carve to both a side view and a front view, the carving just gets too squarish, losing its life-like quality. Second, by using only the profile, there is room for creativity within the carving. Many times I am working on a figure, and it begins to take on a life and personality of its own. I love it when that happens, and I believe that if I were to use patterns from two views it would happen far less often.

So I hope you enjoy this book and that it is a good resource for you. If you need any information about carving, I would suggest that you get a copy of one of my other books. I've tried to fill them with the information you will need to develop your skill and enjoyment in this great hobby!

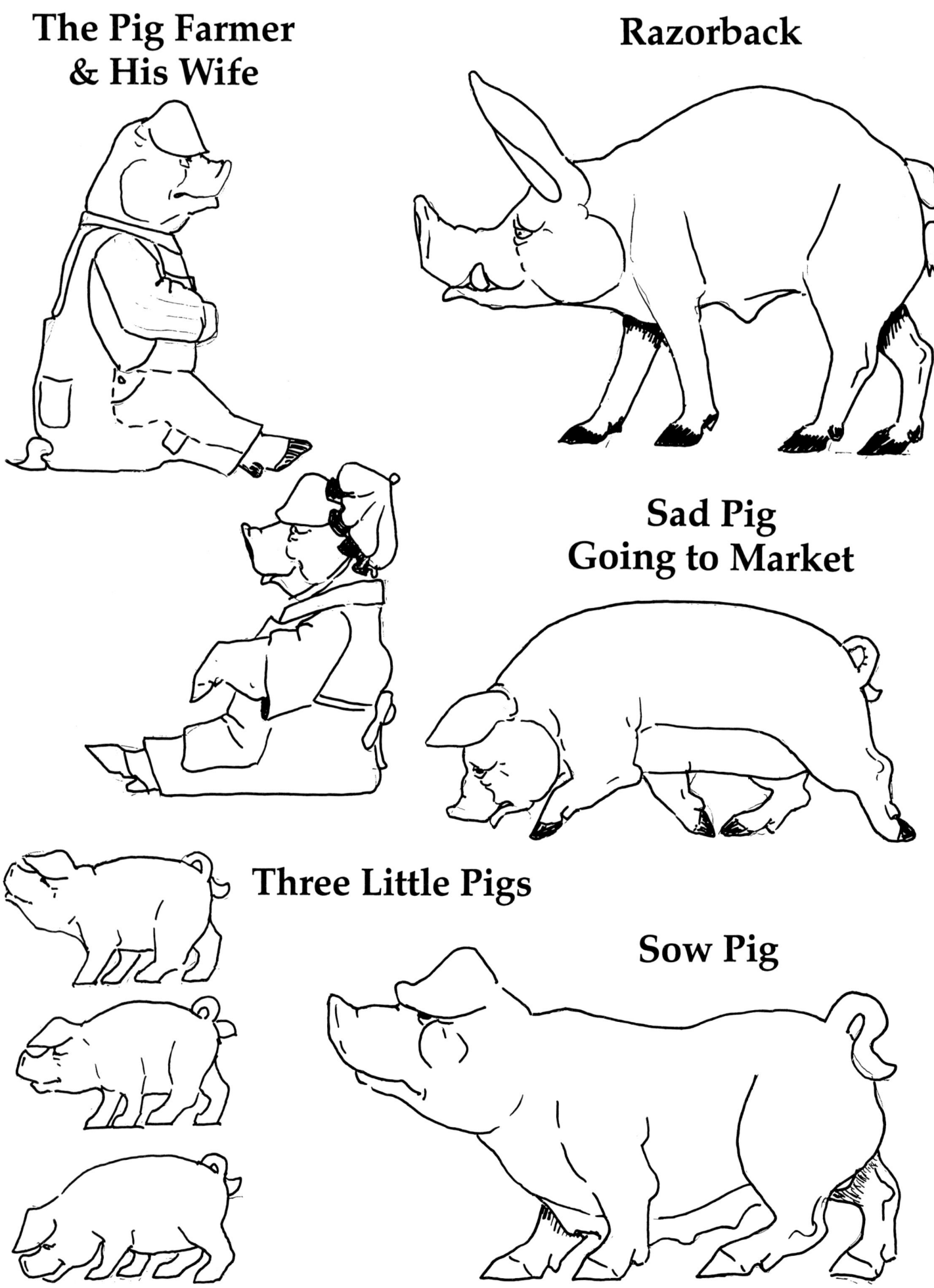

The Pig Farmer
& His Wife

Razorback

Sad Pig
Going to Market

Three Little Pigs

Sow Pig

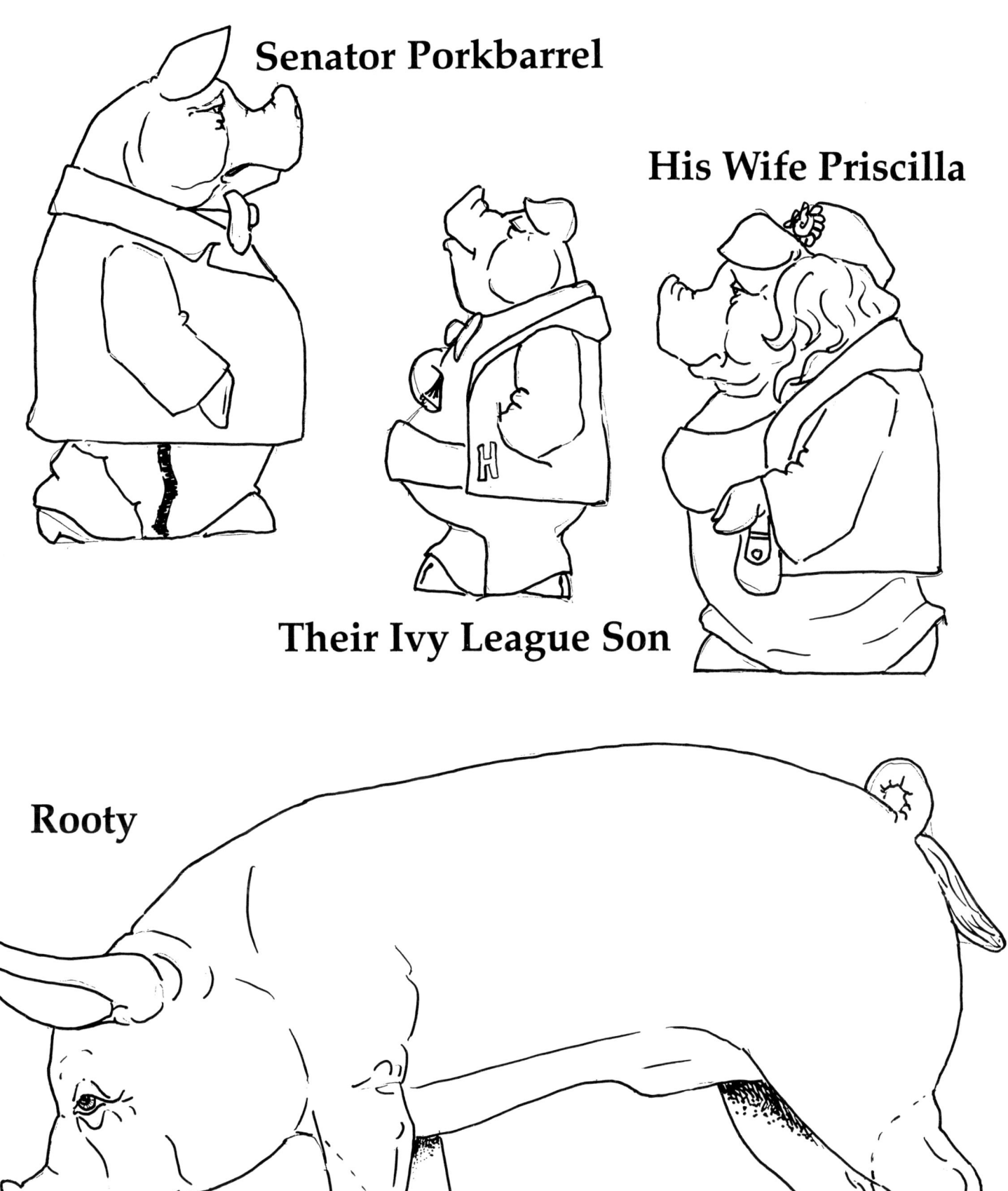

Senator Porkbarrel

His Wife Priscilla

Their Ivy League Son

Rooty

# Friendly Bob

# The Ramped Rooter

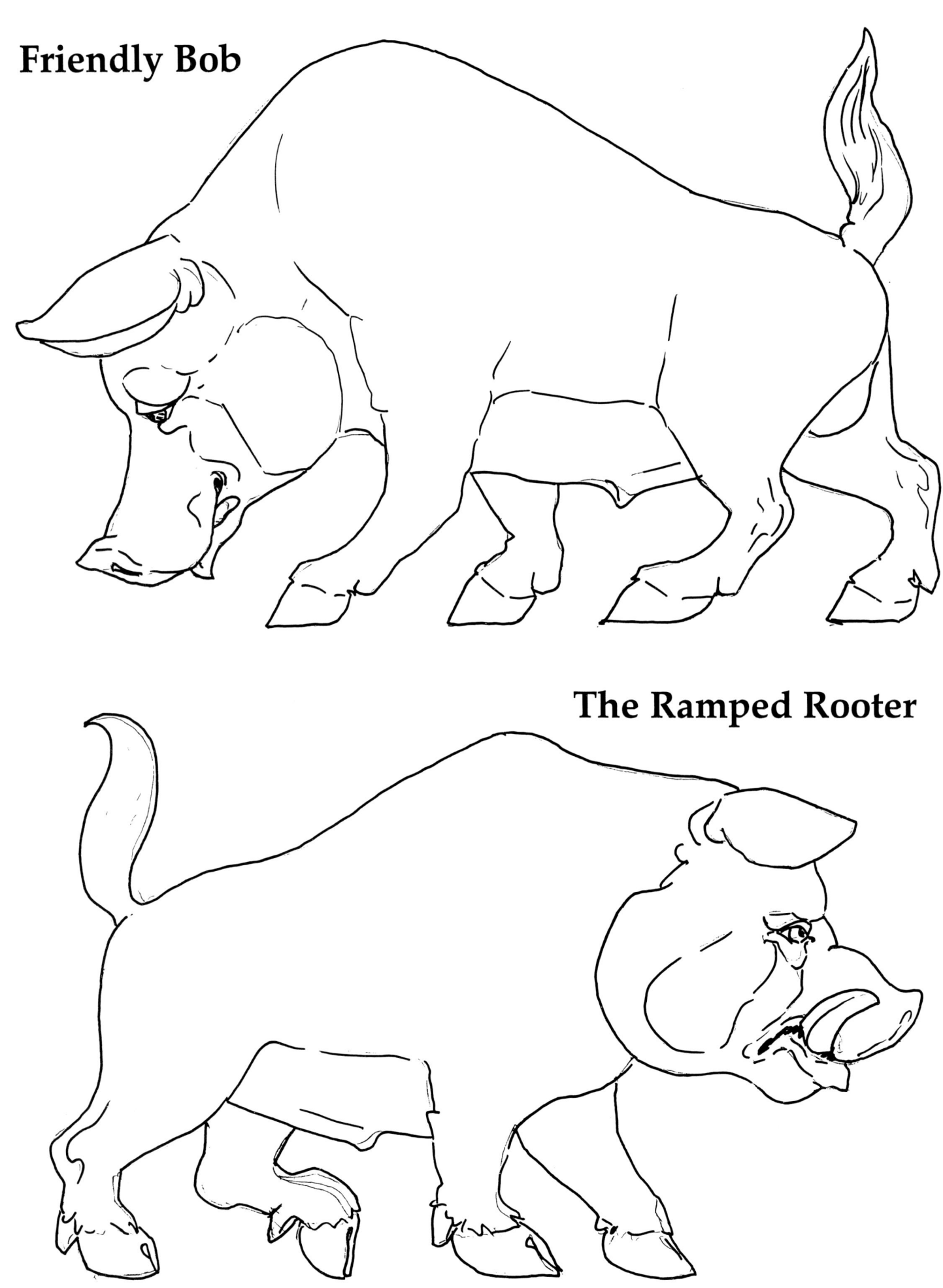

# Old Snort

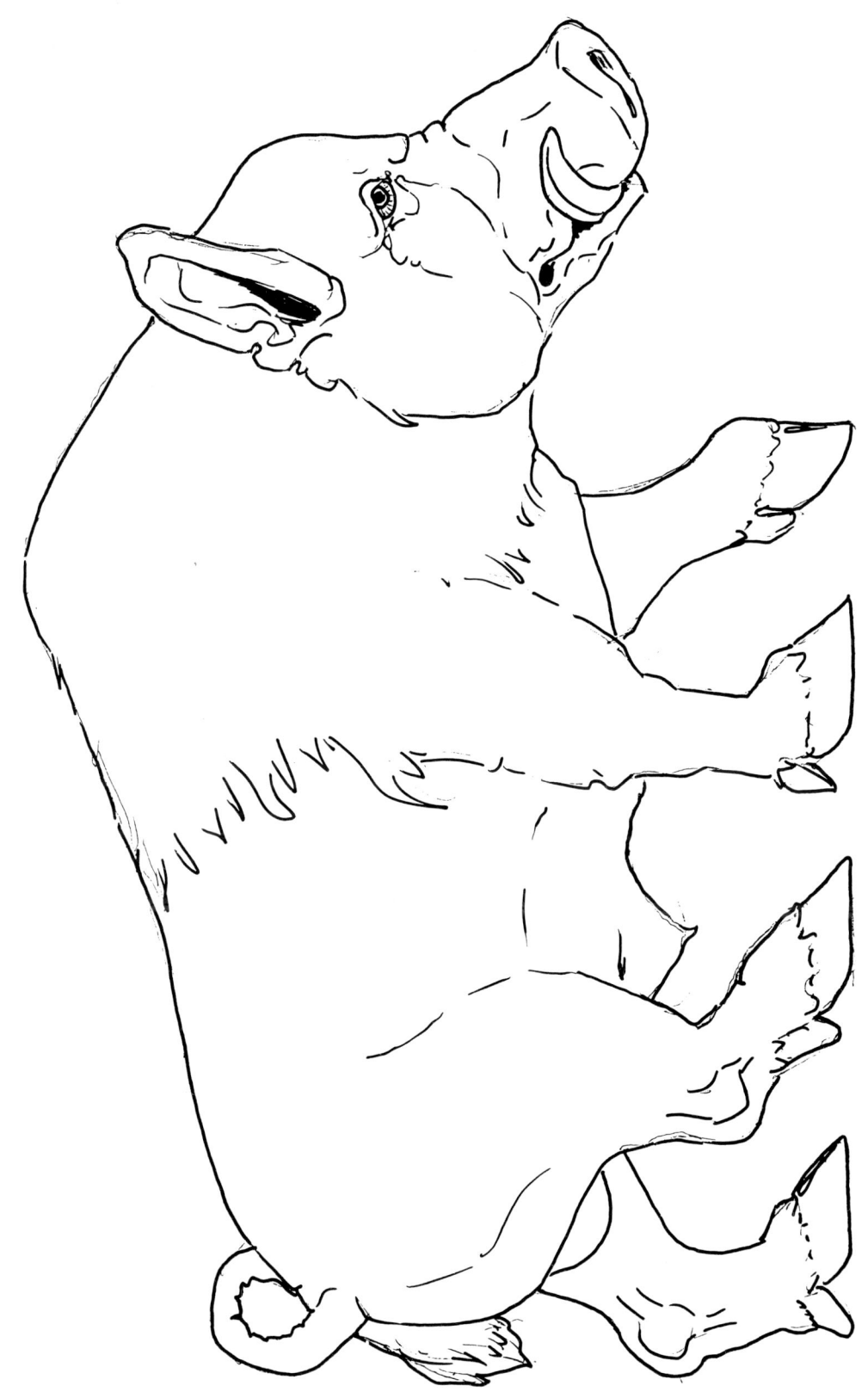

# Bush Hog

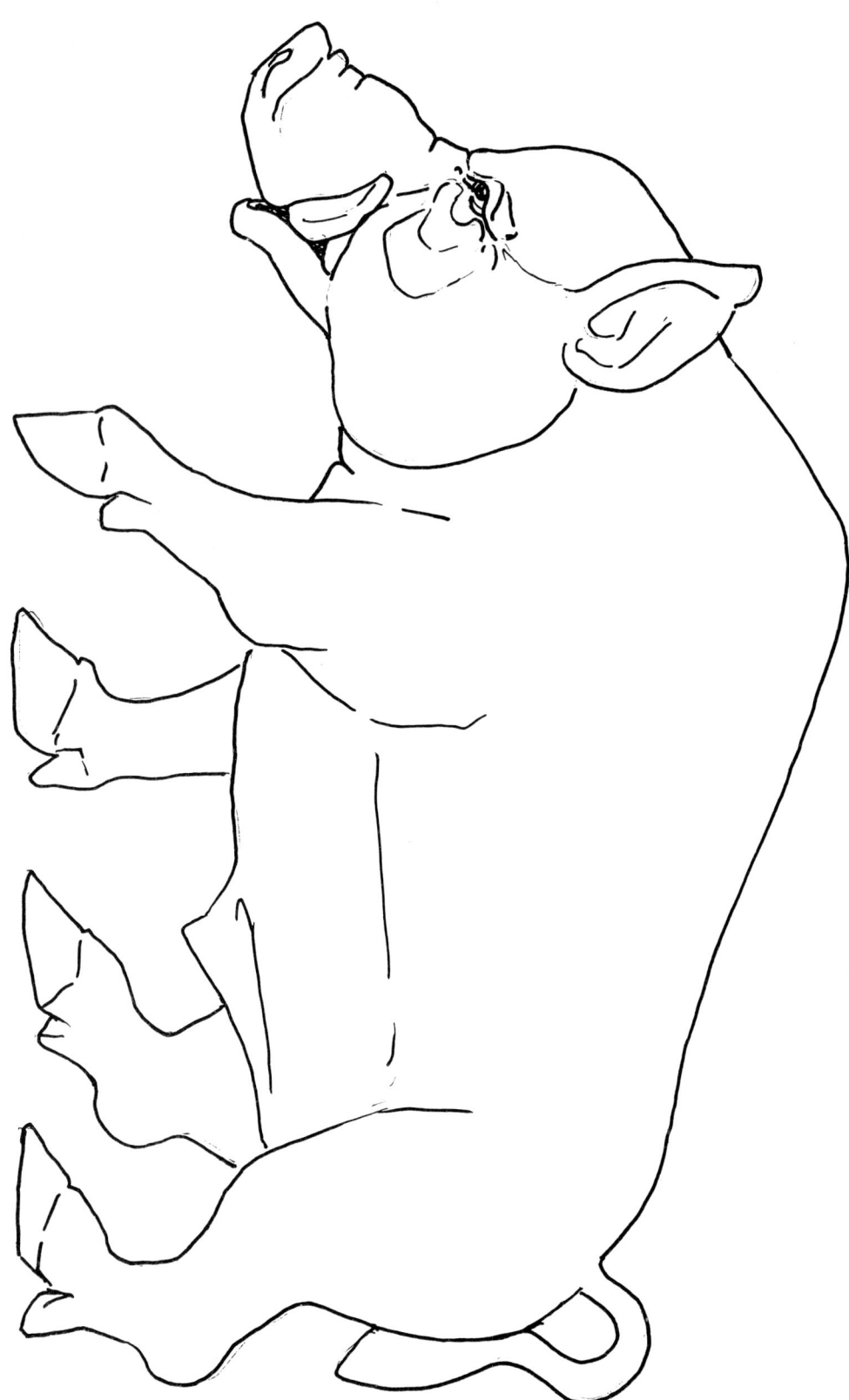

# Corn Finder

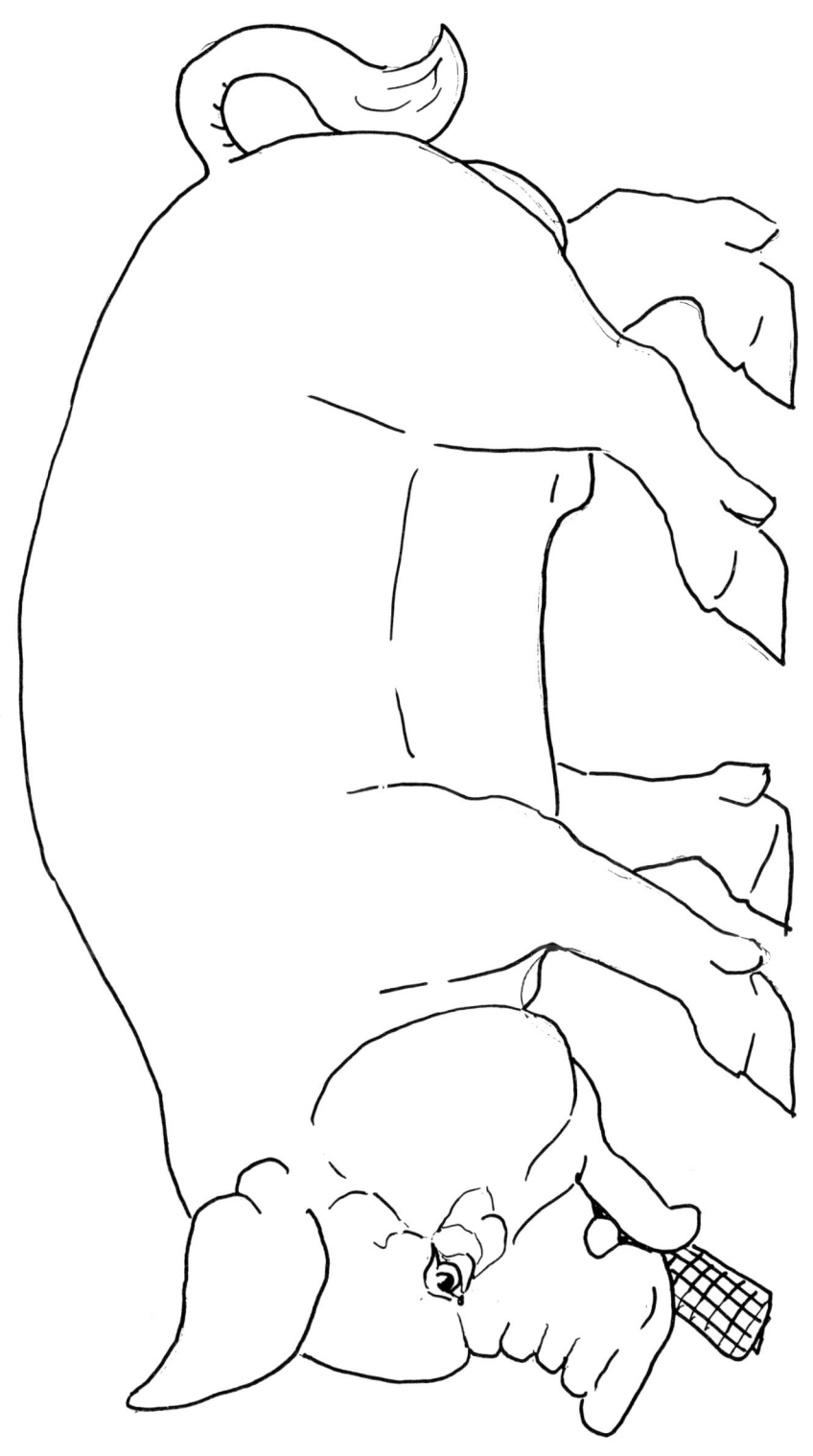

# Opossum

There's an old southern fable, "If you hold an
opossum up to your ear you
can hear the highway!"

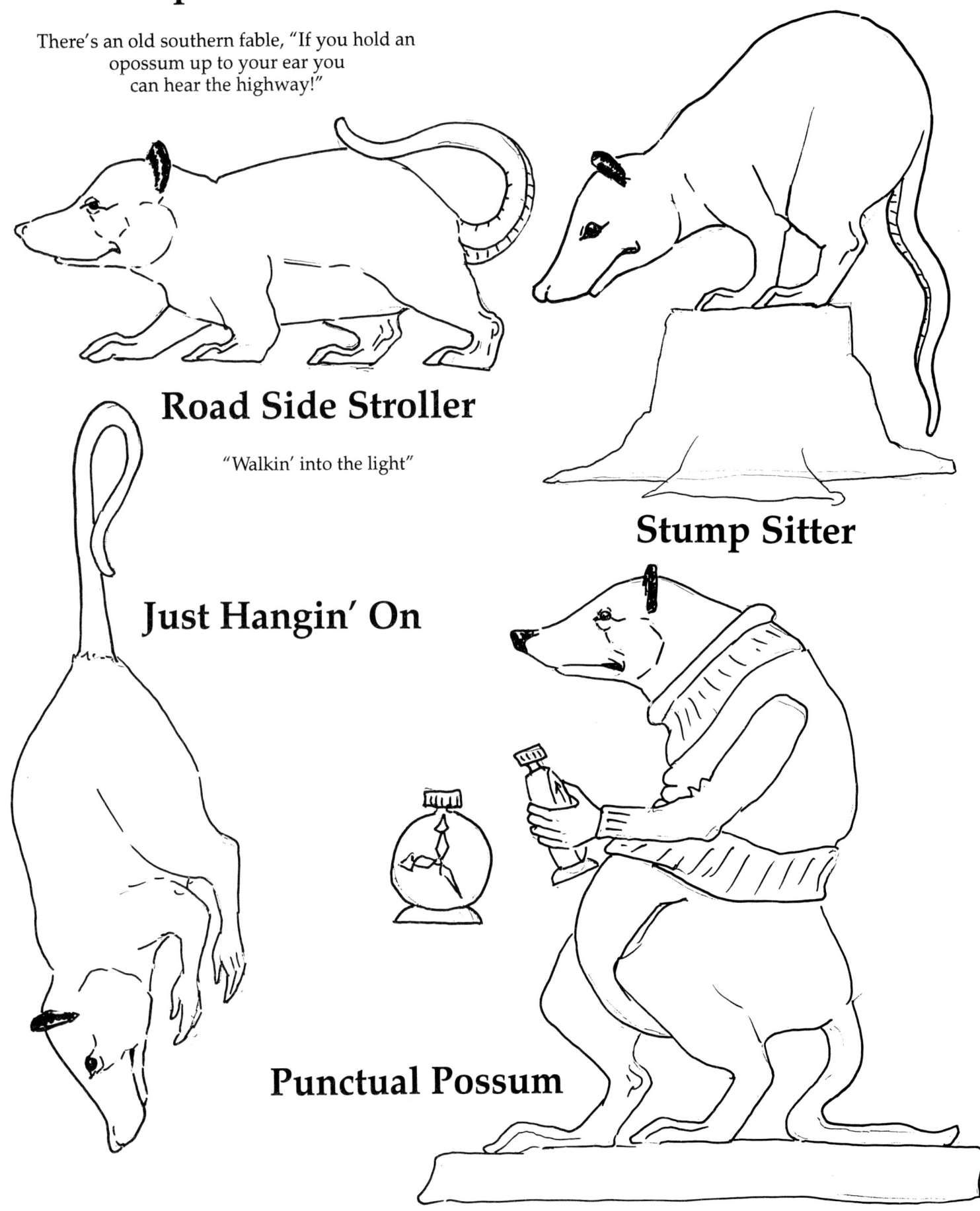

## Road Side Stroller

*"Walkin' into the light"*

## Stump Sitter

## Just Hangin' On

## Punctual Possum

# Pussy Cats

This page is dedicated to my
old pit bull "Dutch." She loved cats.

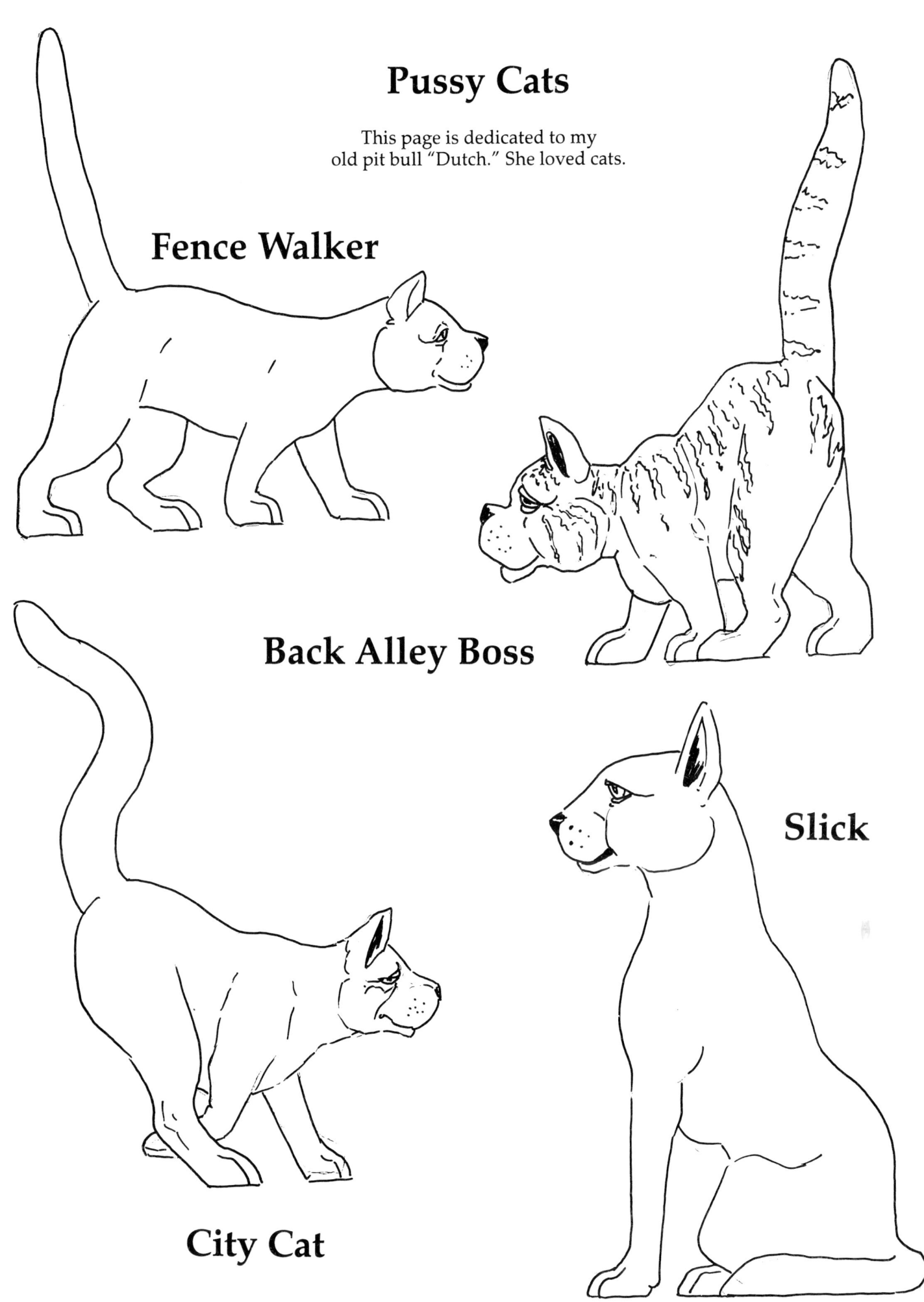

**Fence Walker**

**Back Alley Boss**

**Slick**

**City Cat**

# The Little Rascals

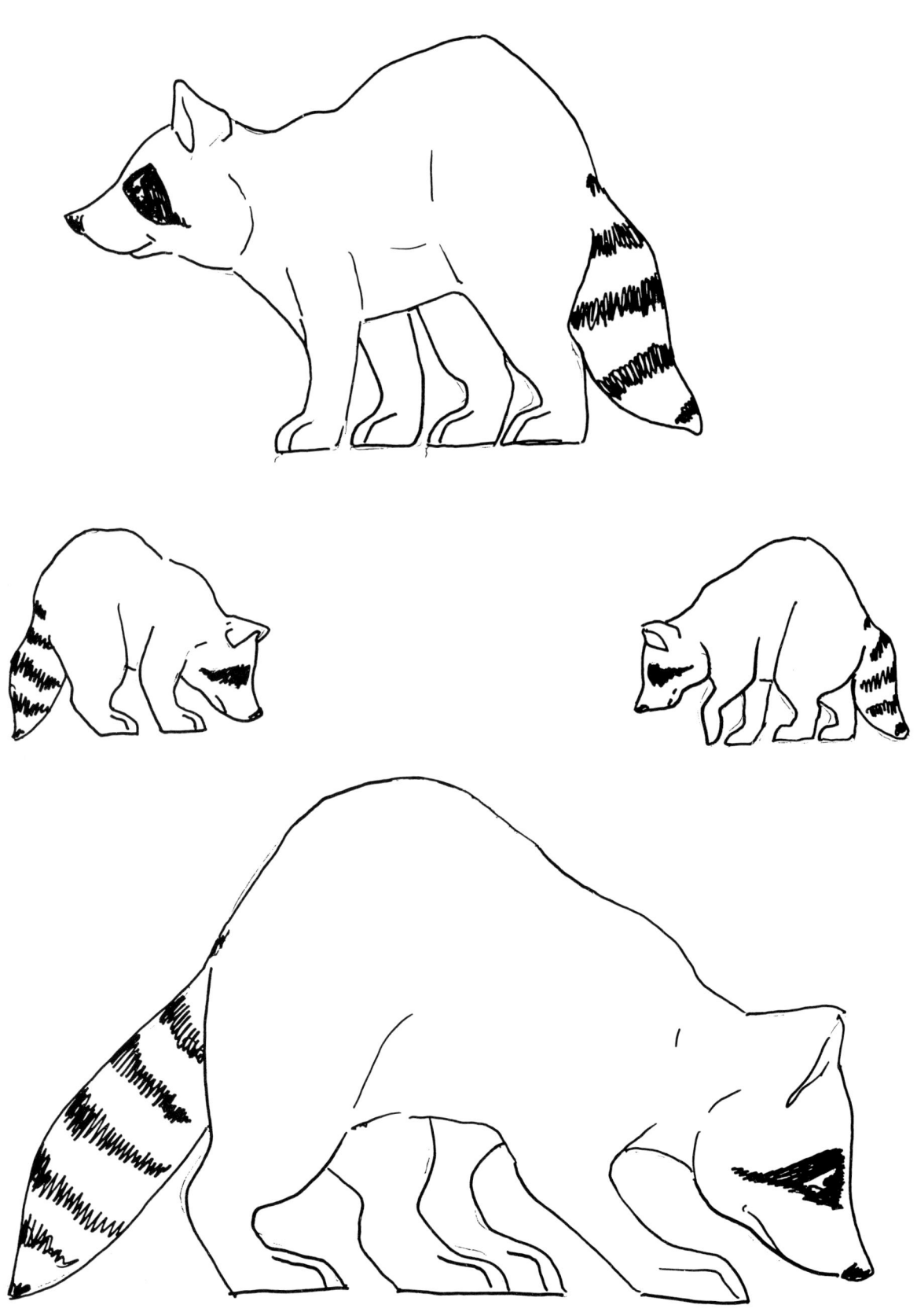

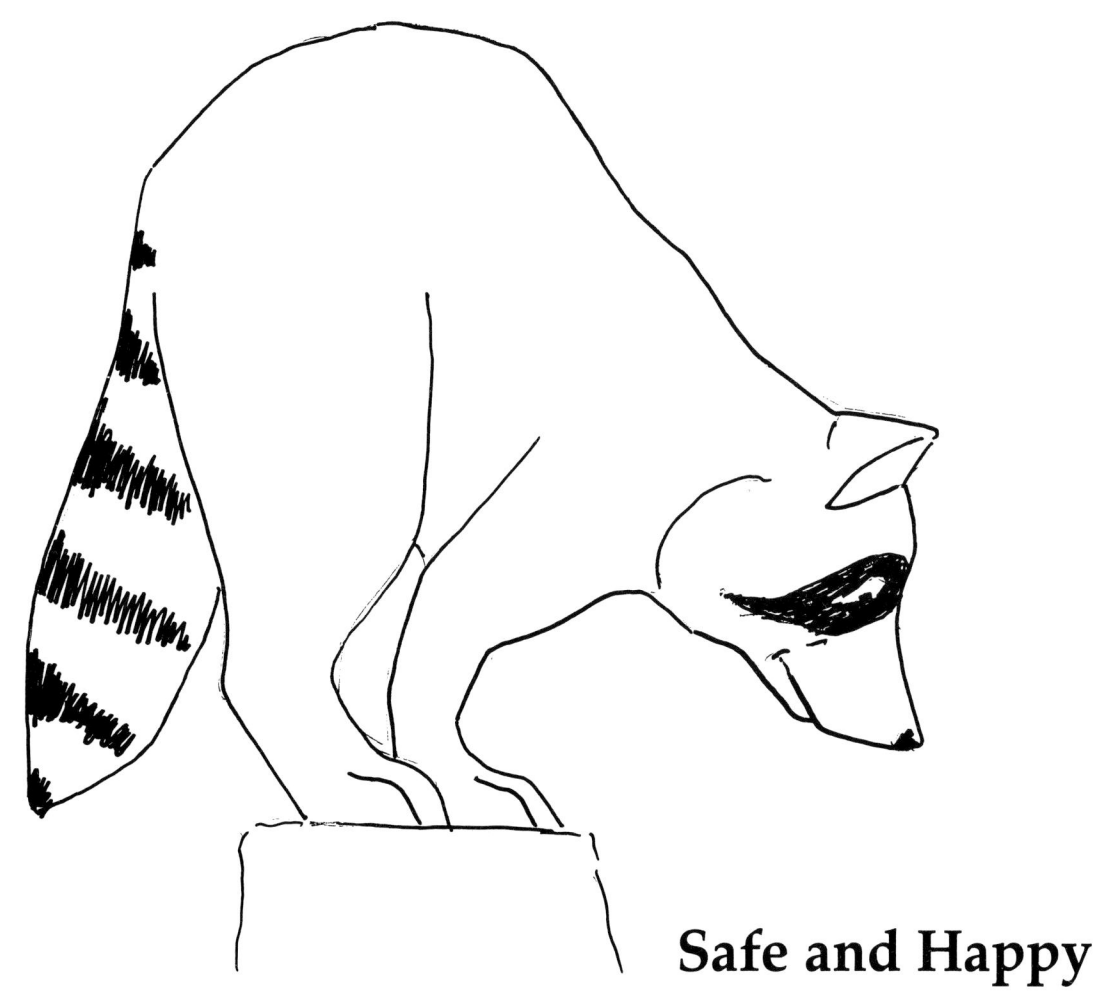

**Safe and Happy**

**Movin' On**

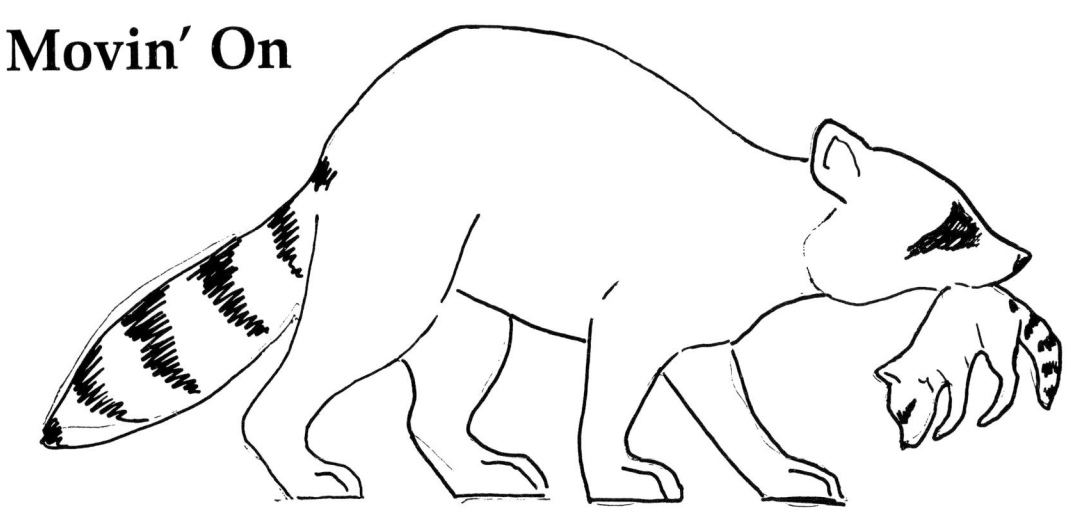

13

**Playtime**

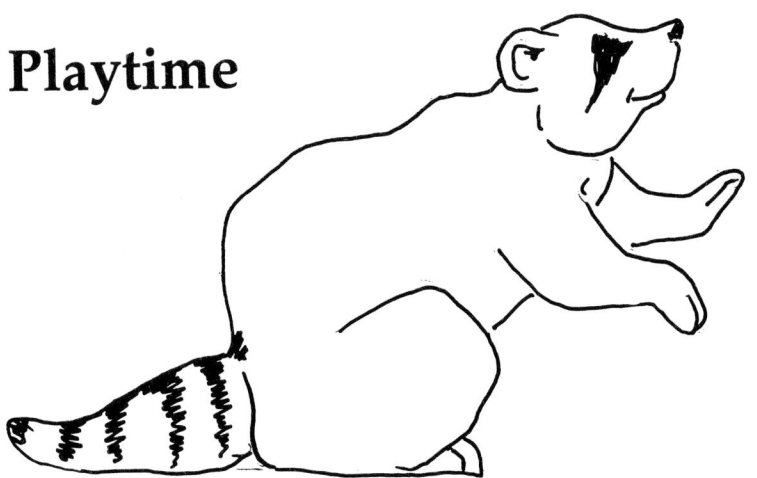

**Looking Down**

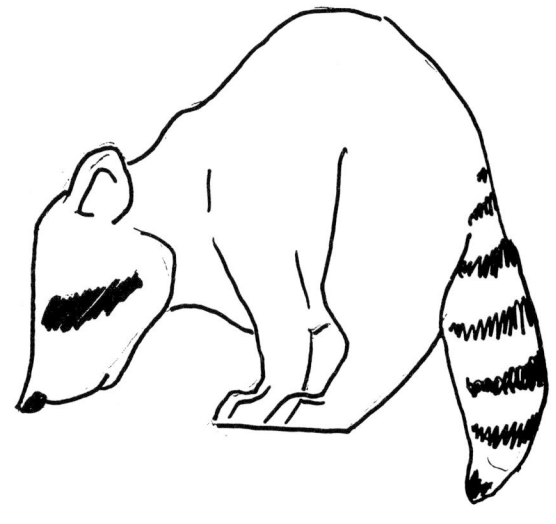

**Deep in Thought**

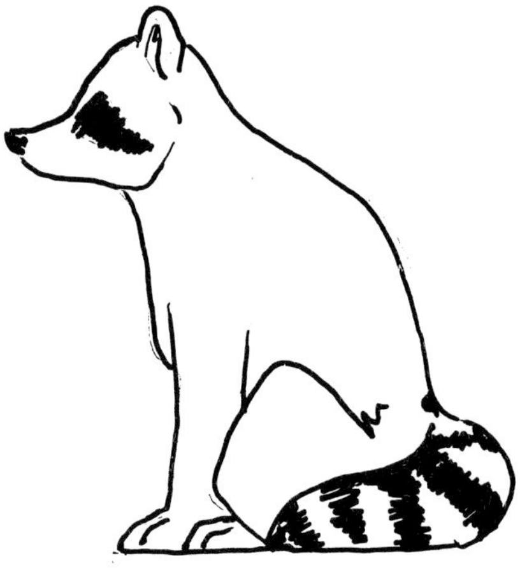

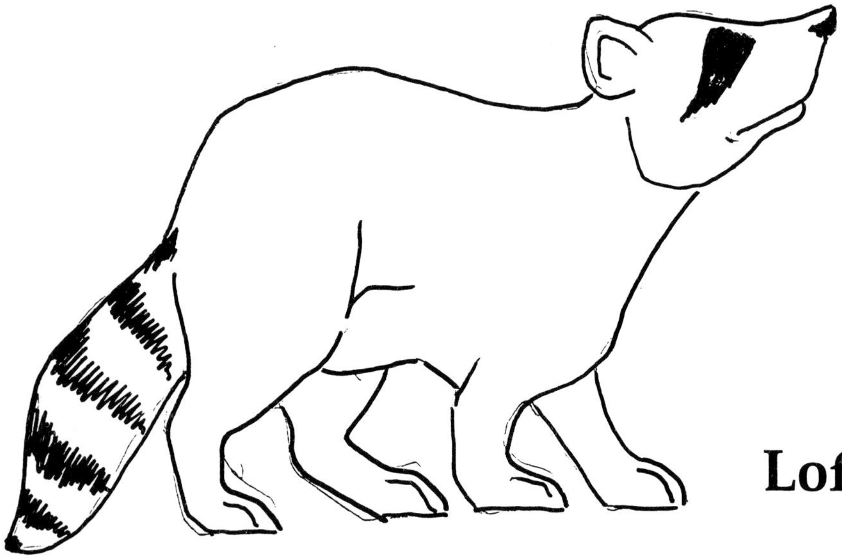

**Lofty Loafer**

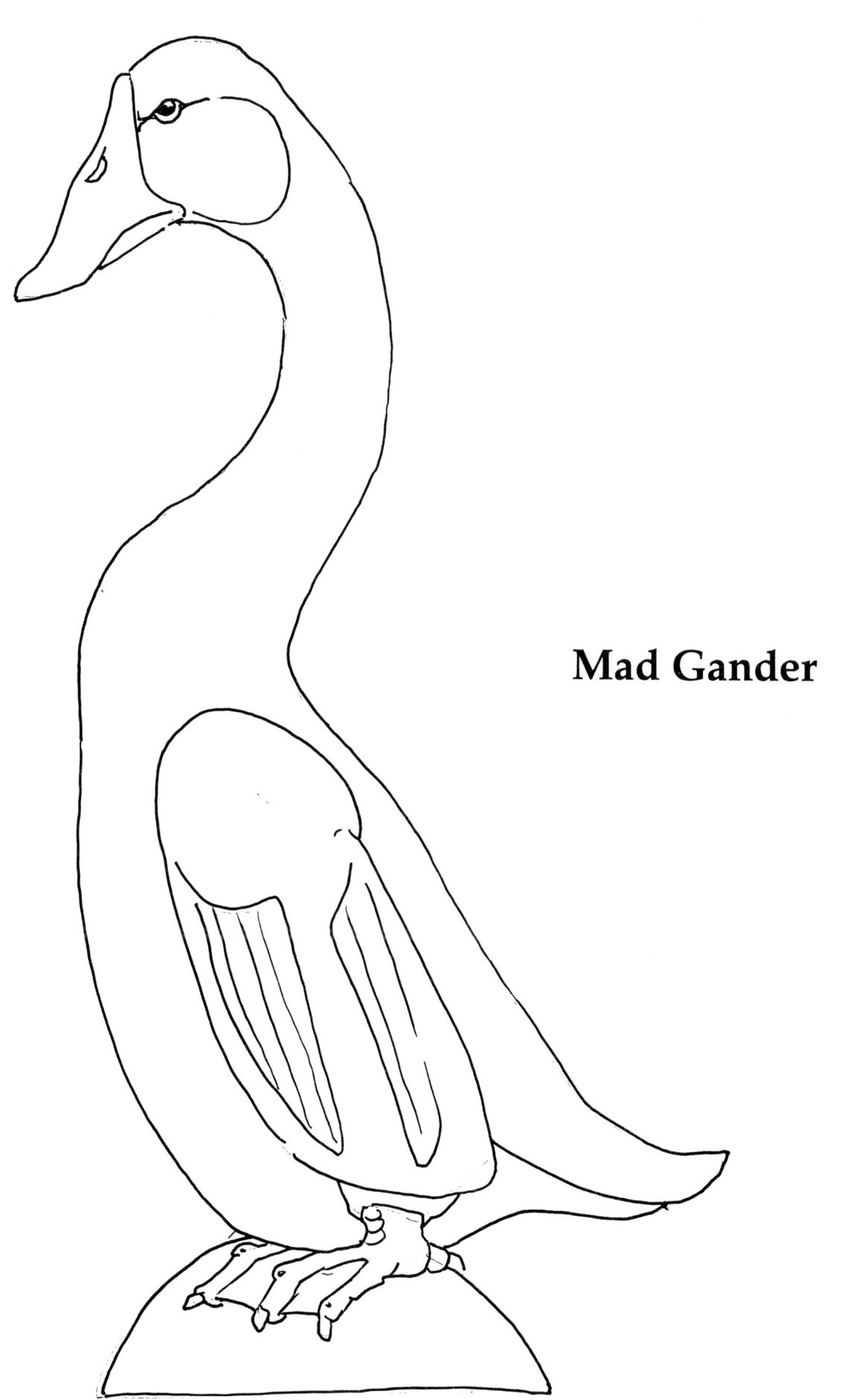

**Mad Gander**

# Clyde

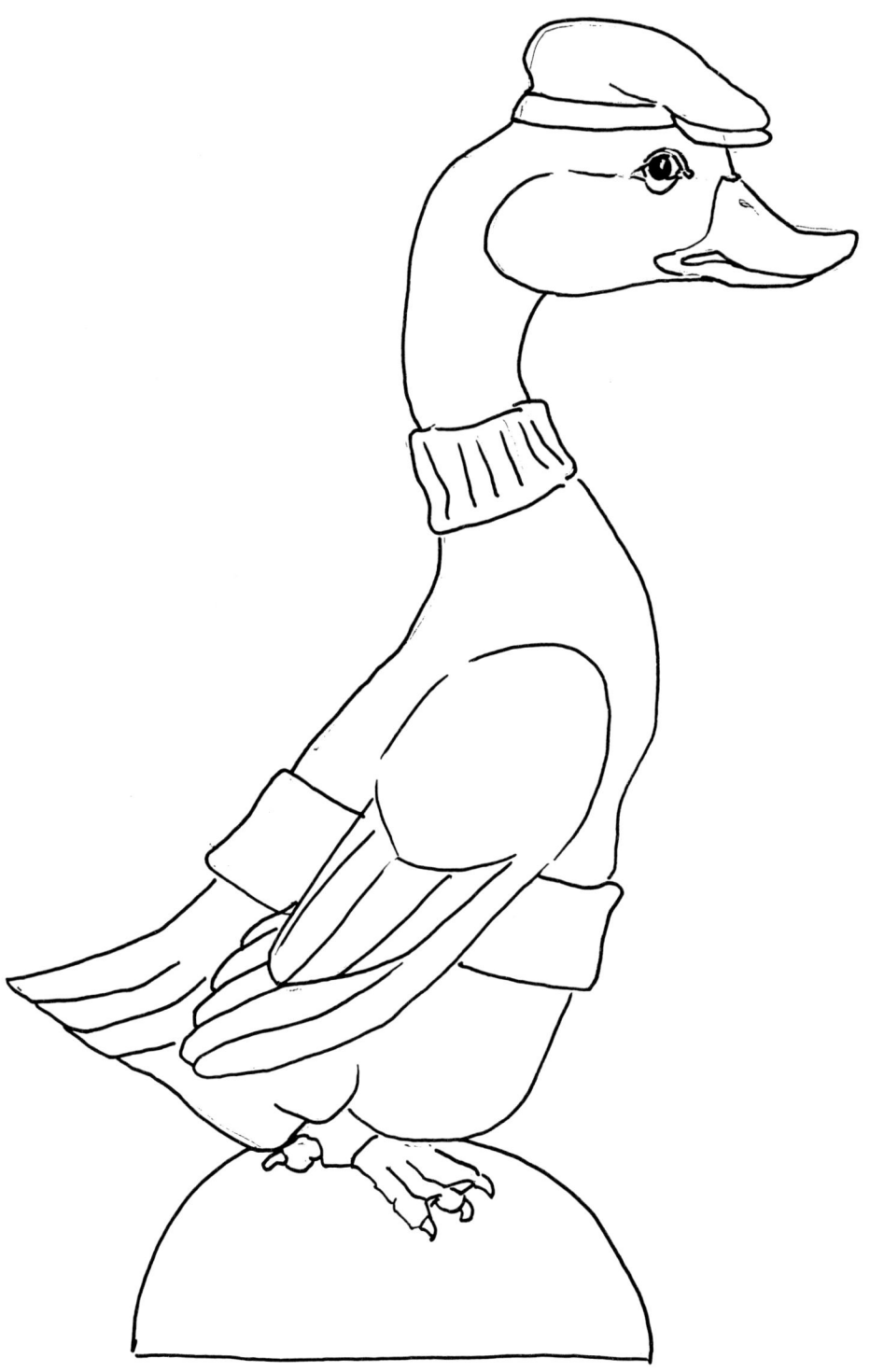

# Bonnie

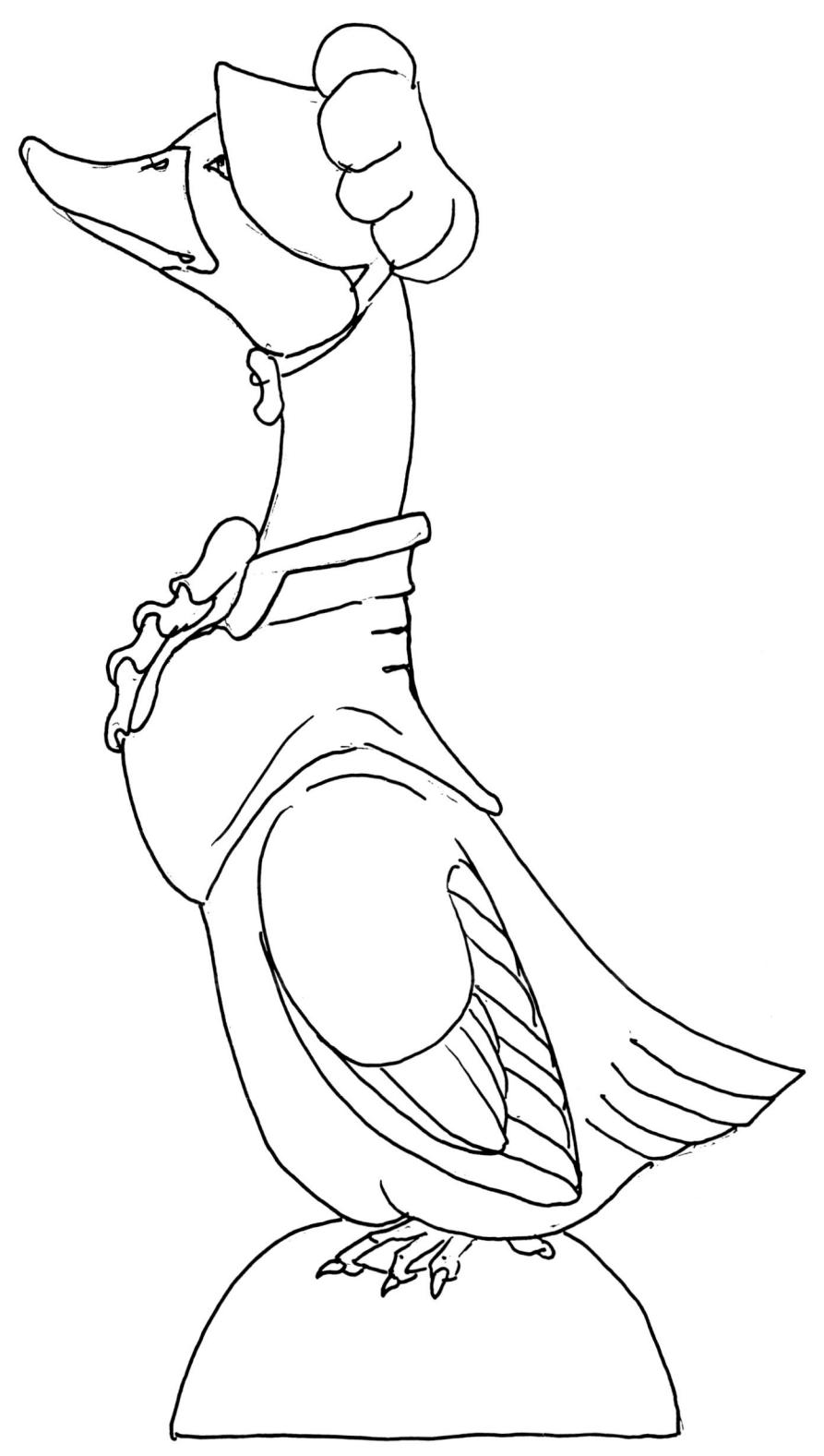

# The Barn Yard Three

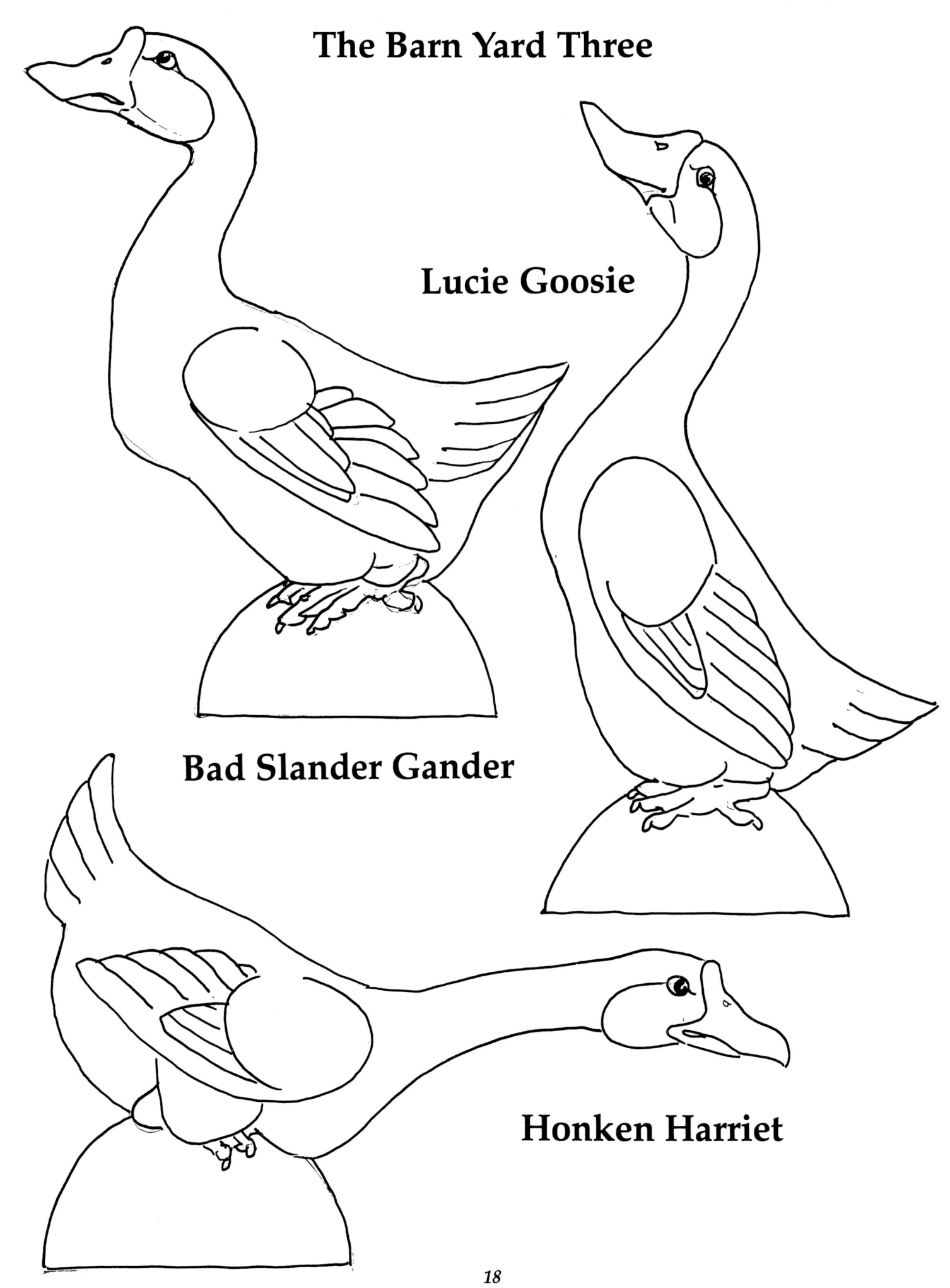

Lucie Goosie

Bad Slander Gander

Honken Harriet

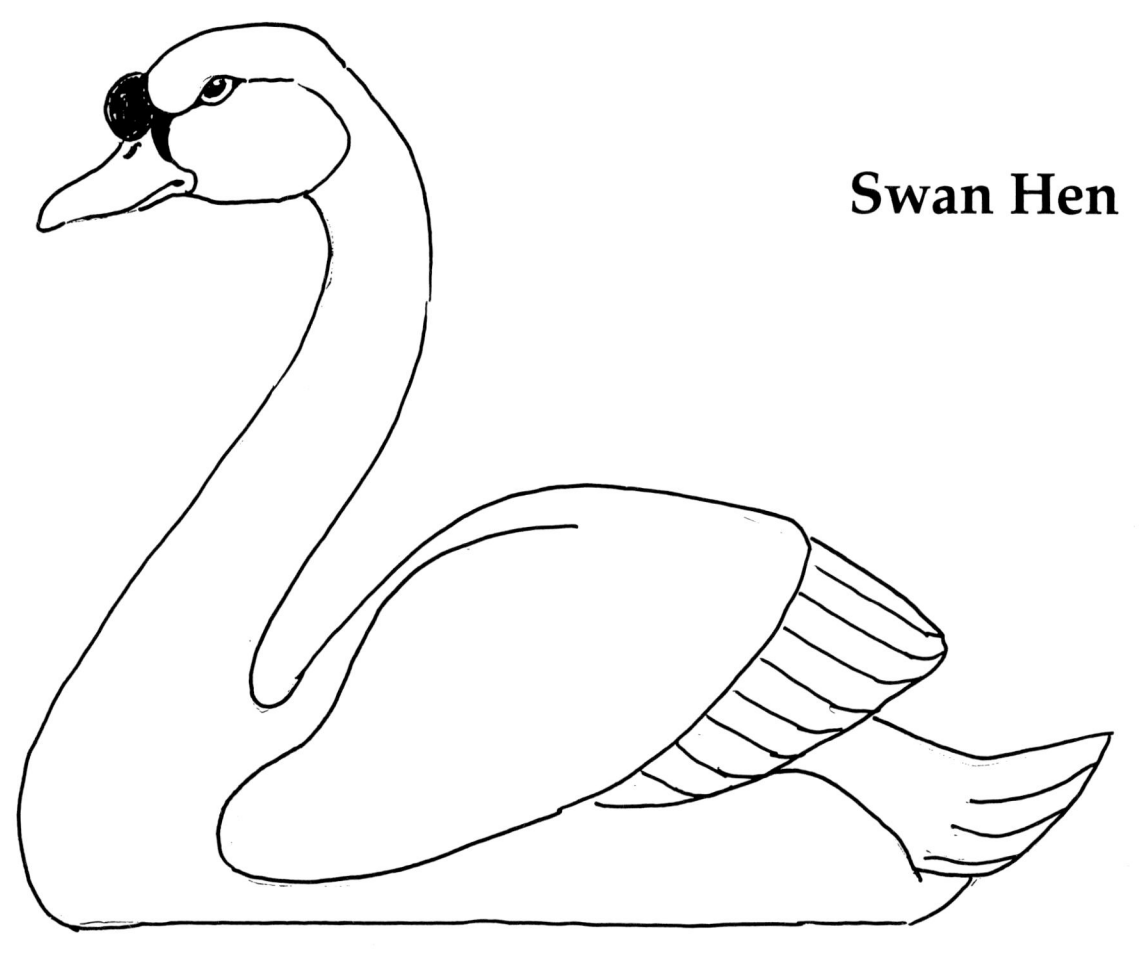

**Swan Hen**

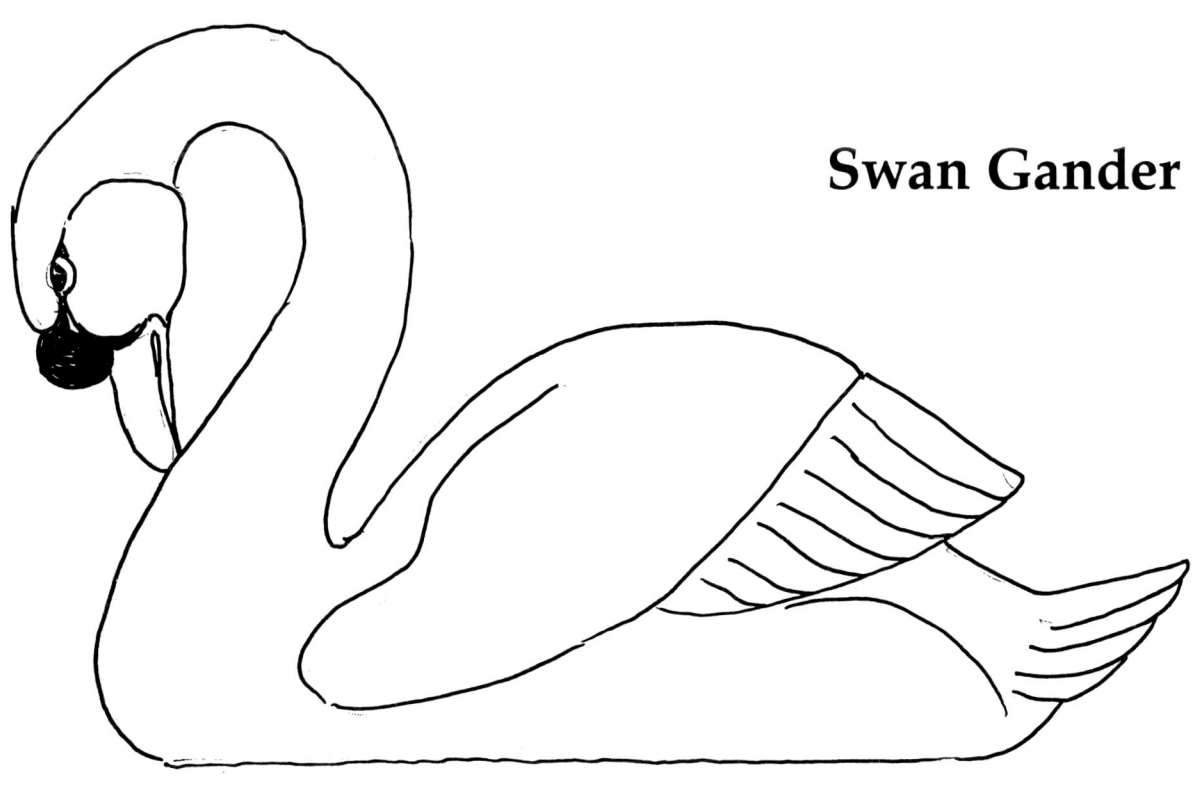

**Swan Gander**

# The Gaggle at the Pond

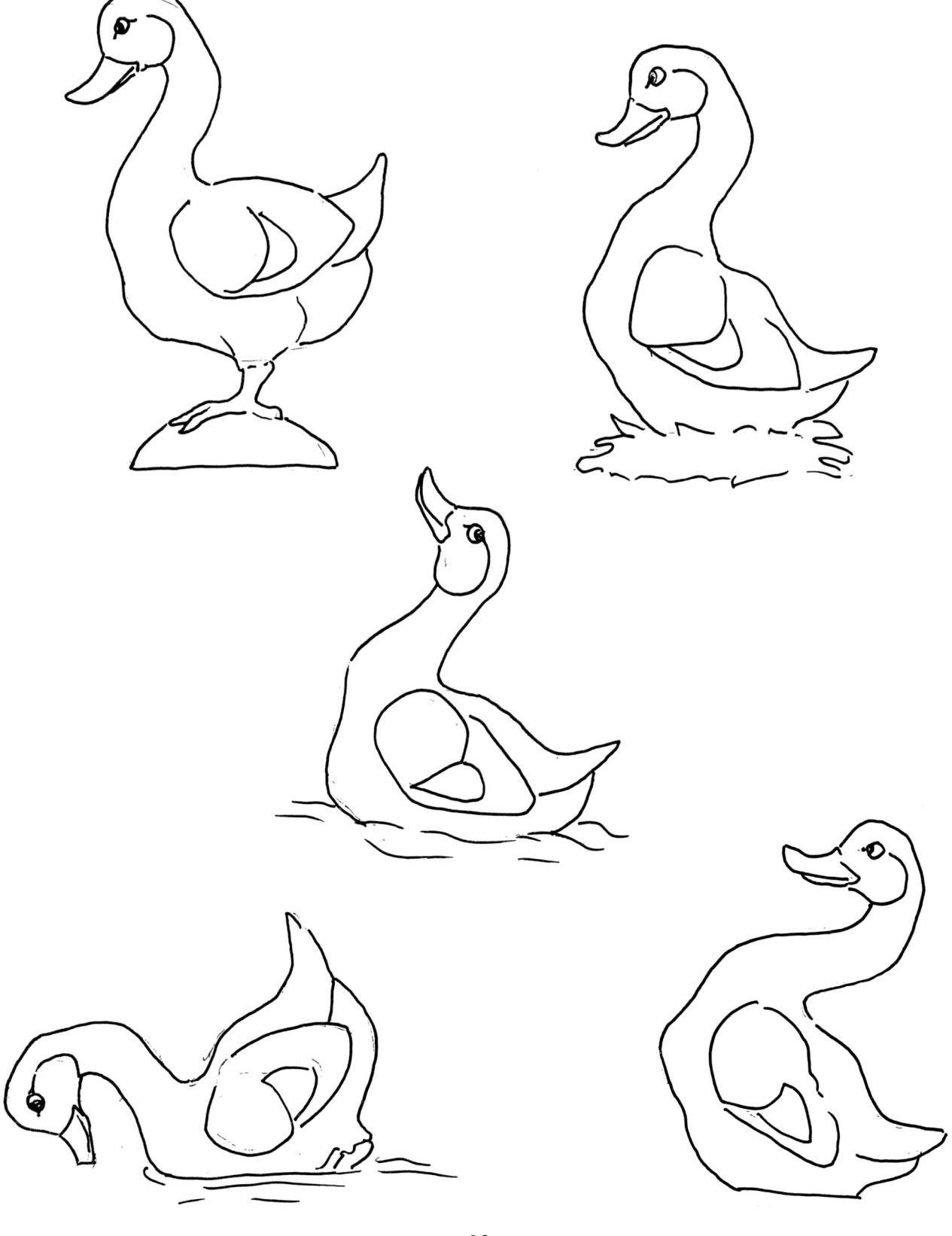

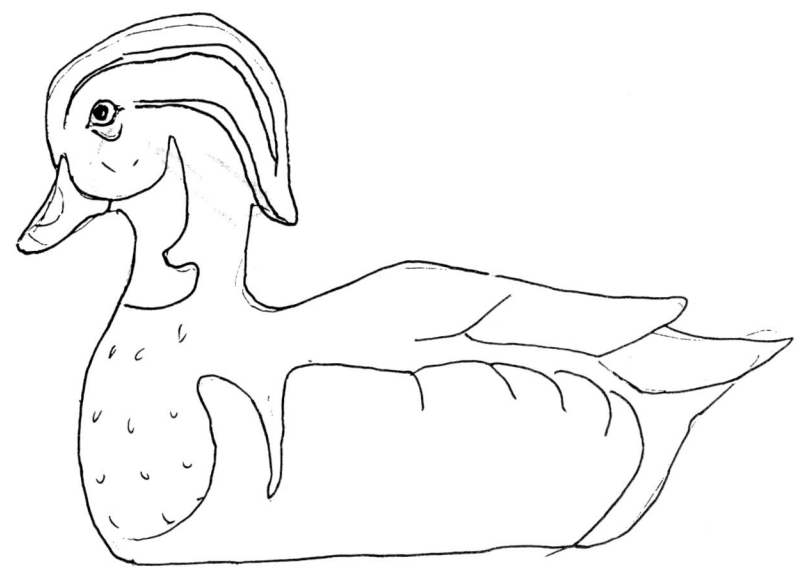

**Woody**

**Mallard**

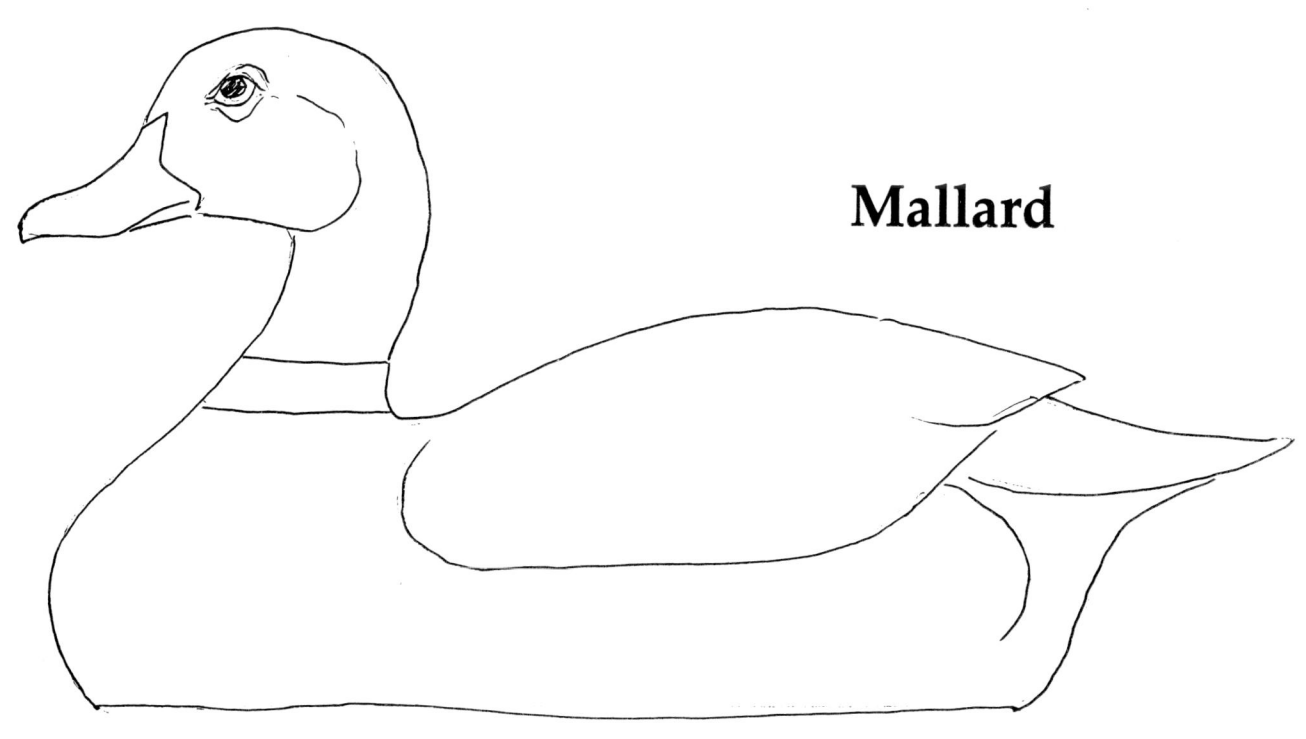

# Papa Bear

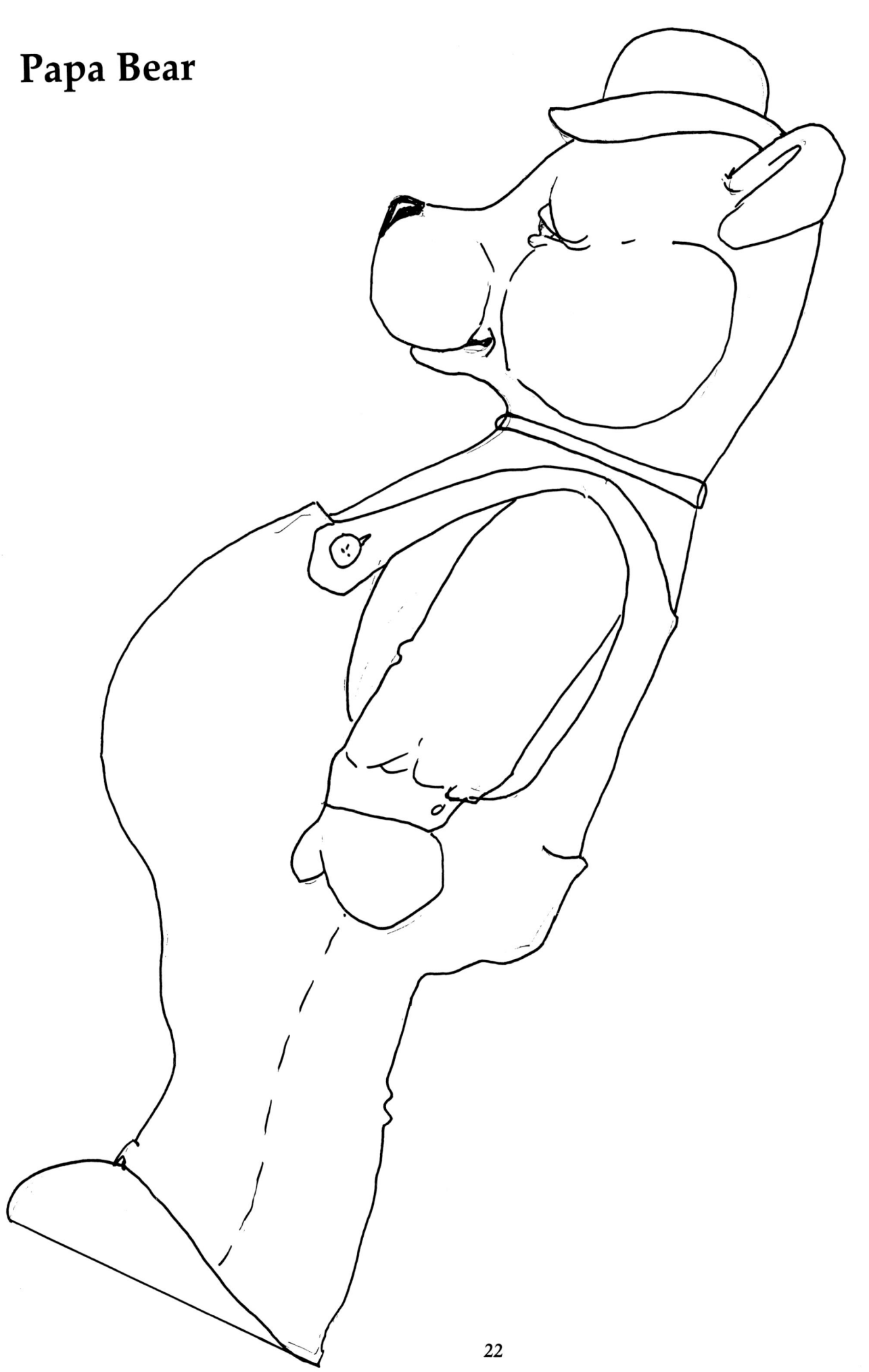

# Mama Bear

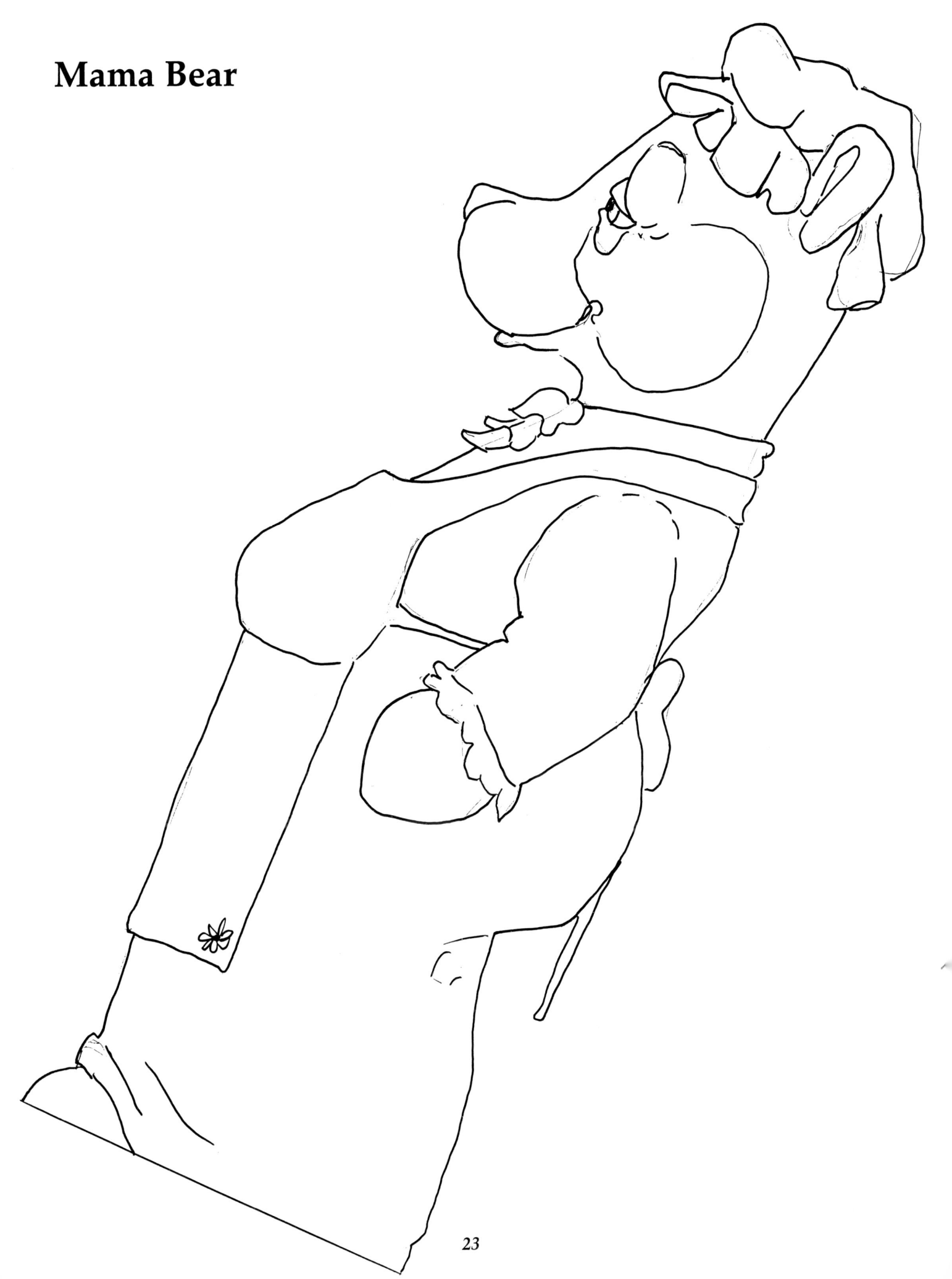

# The Three Baby Bears

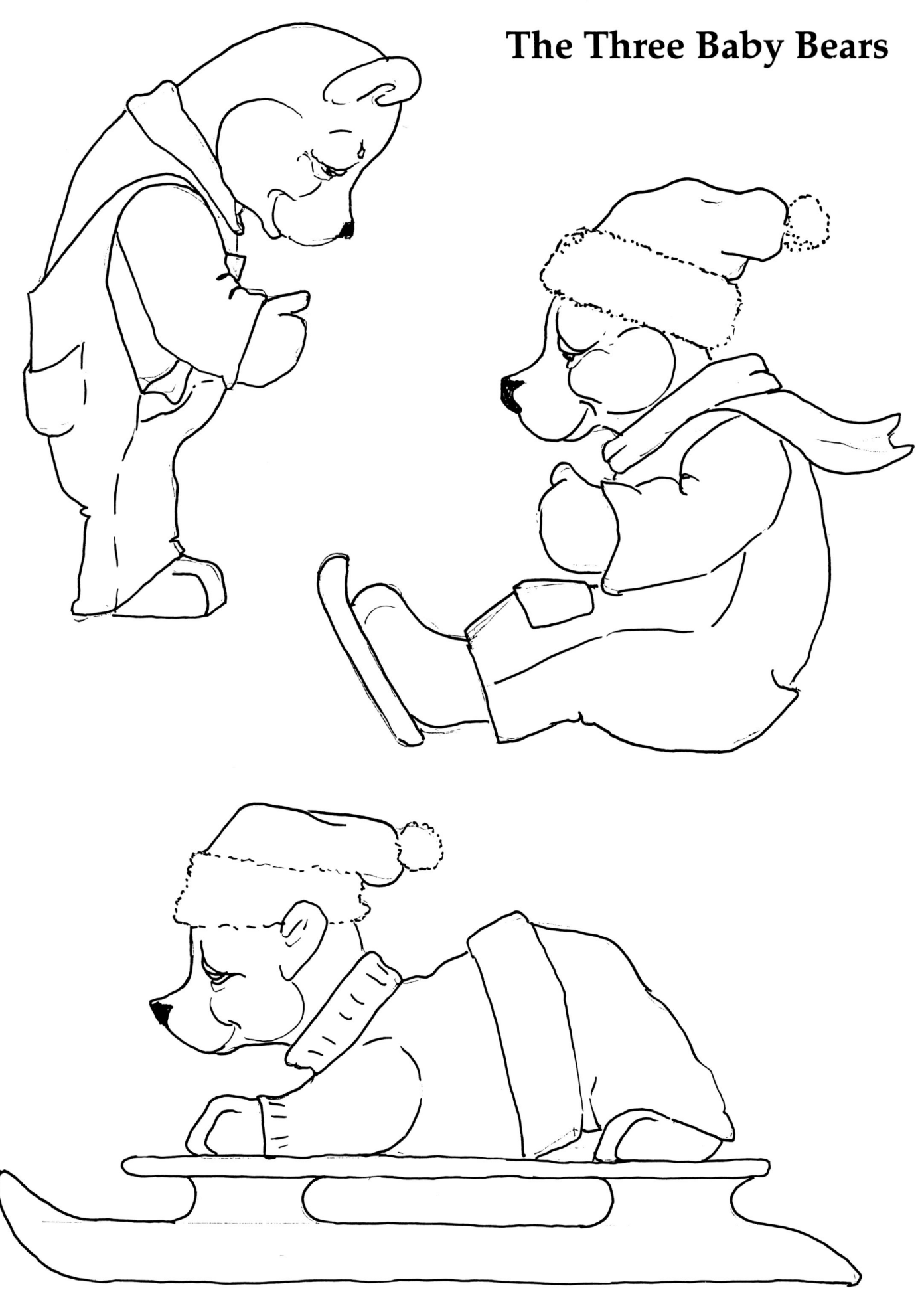

# Rampant Rage

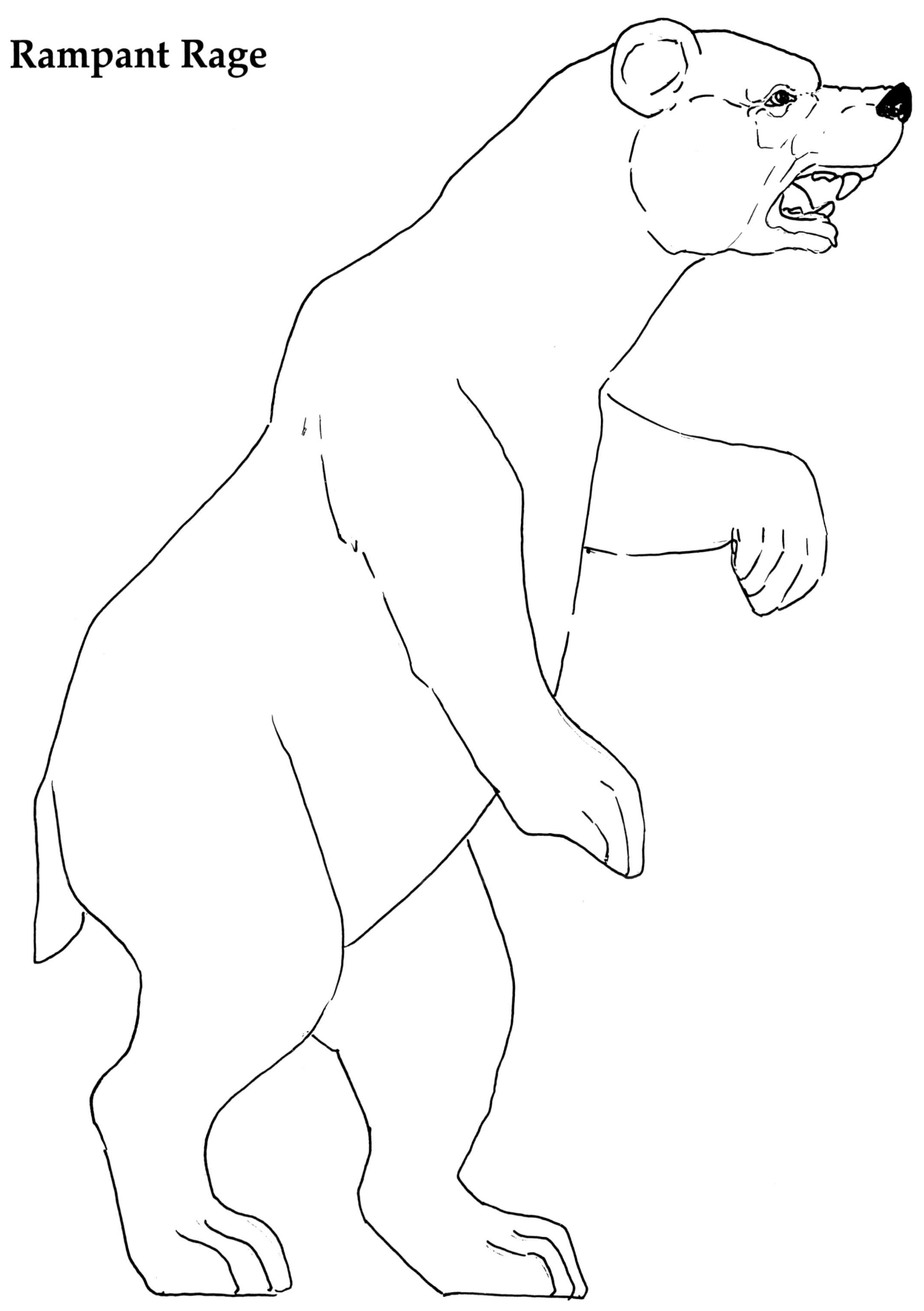

# Mother in Defense

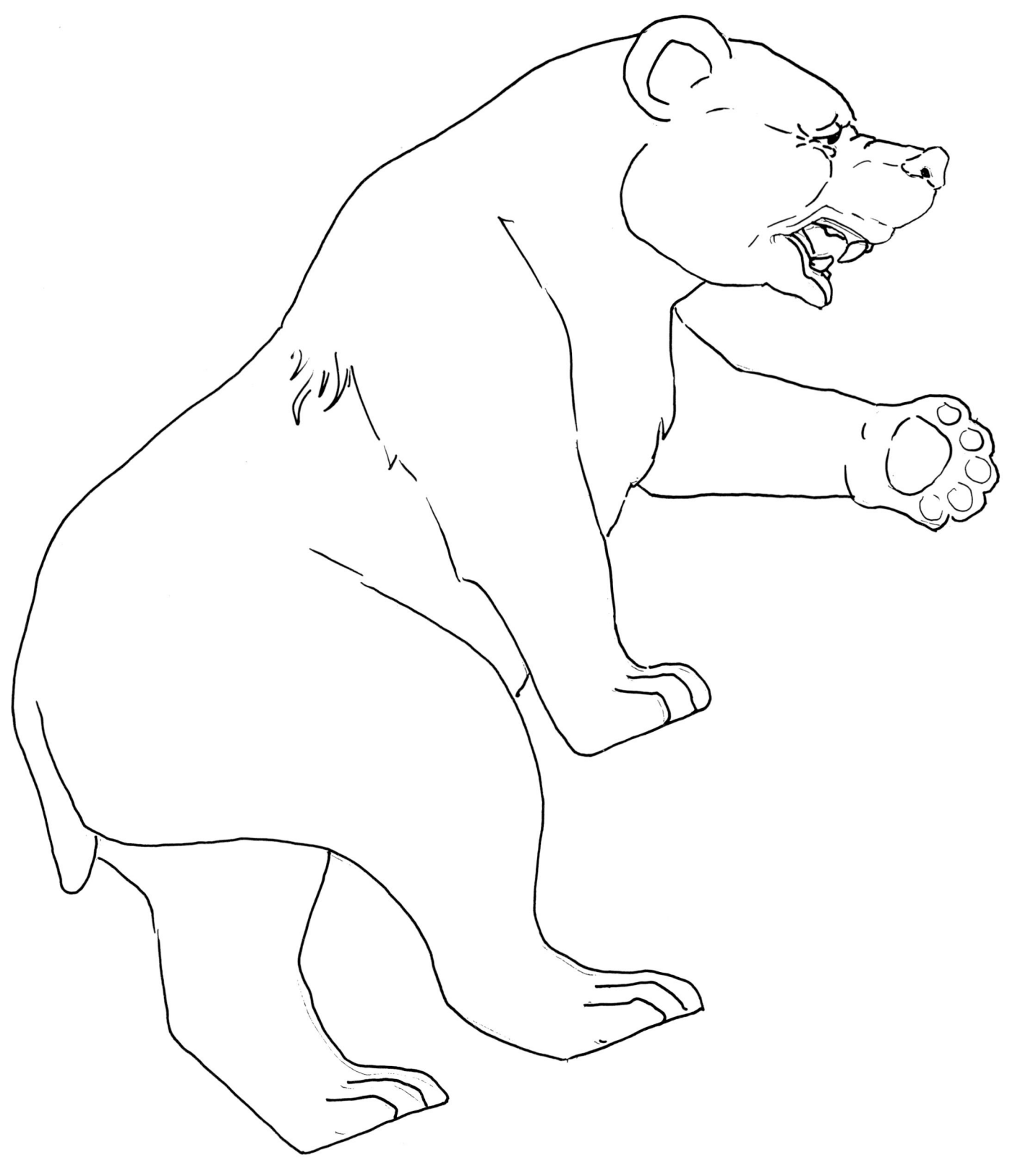

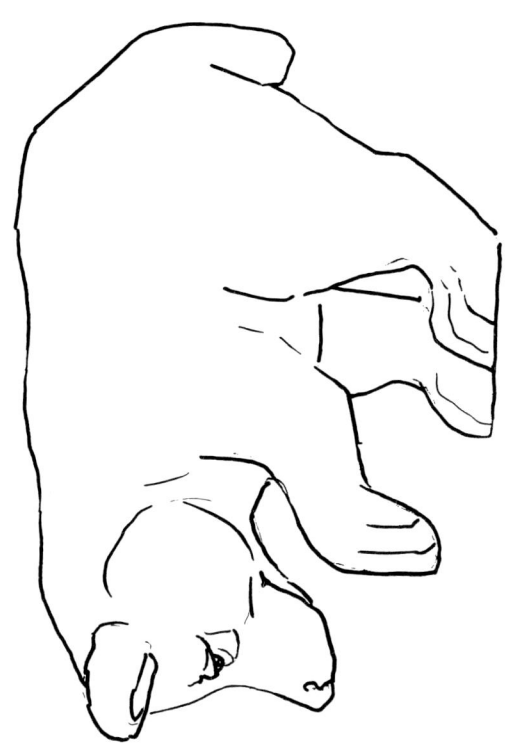

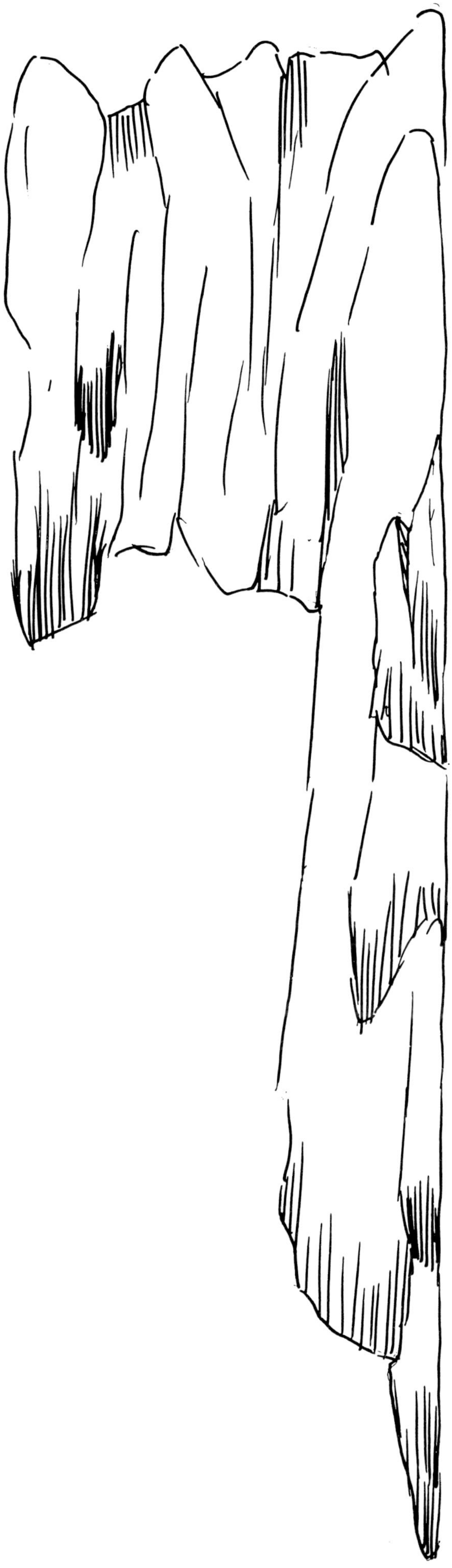

**Cubs**

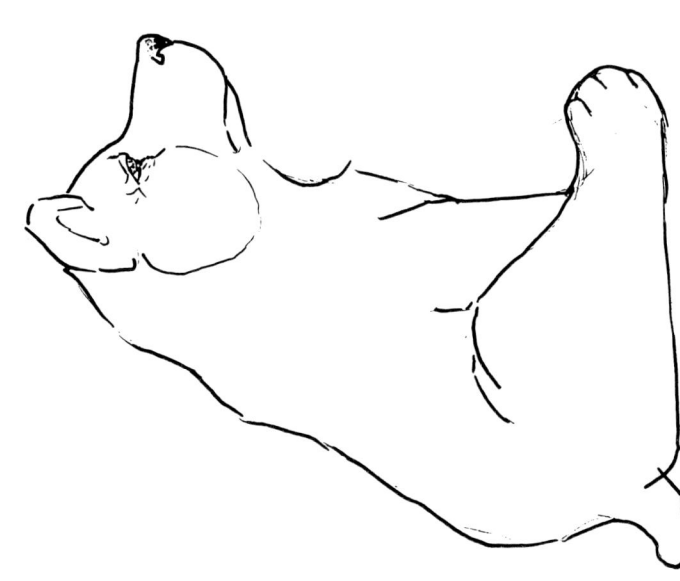

# Moveable Teddy Bear

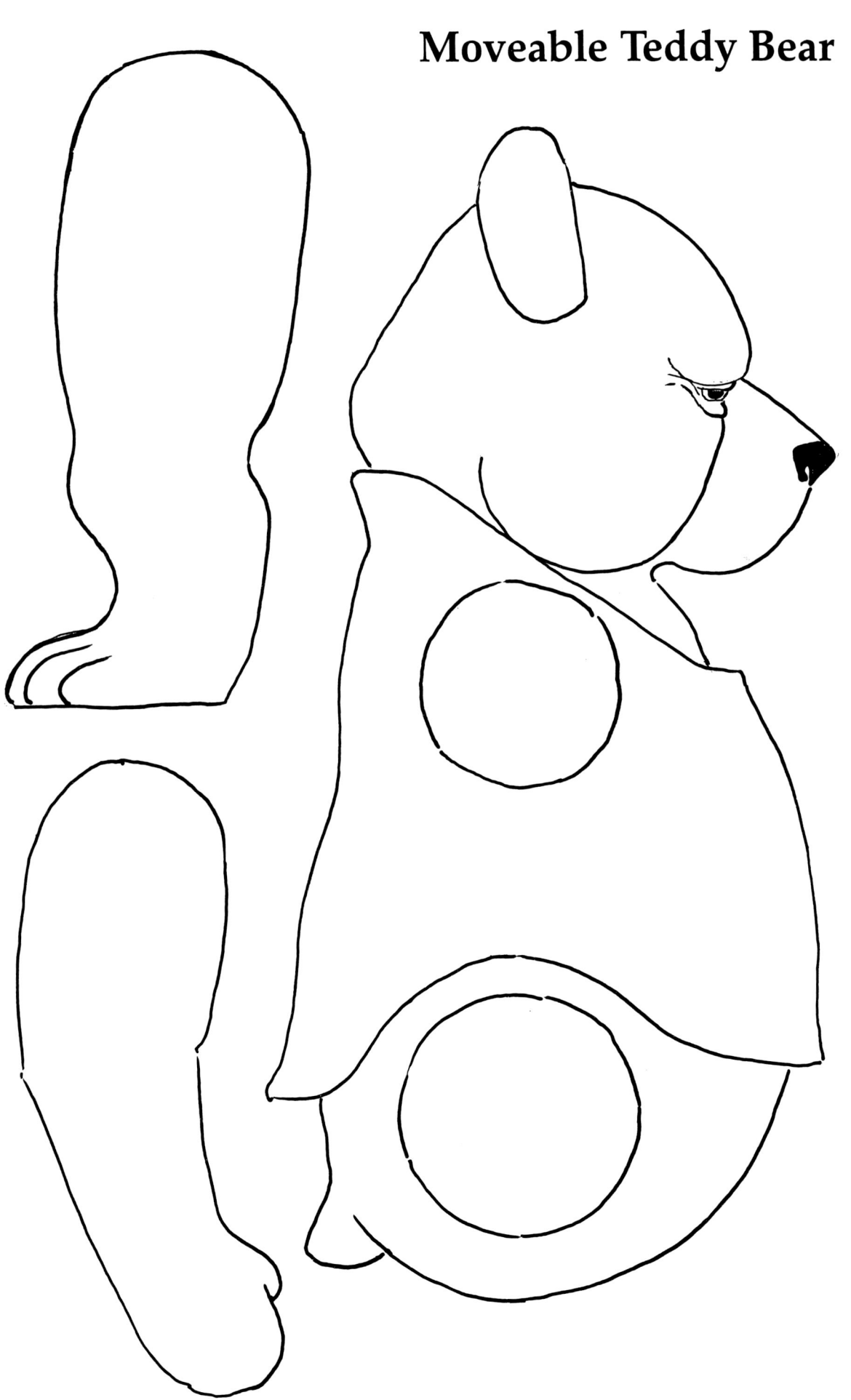

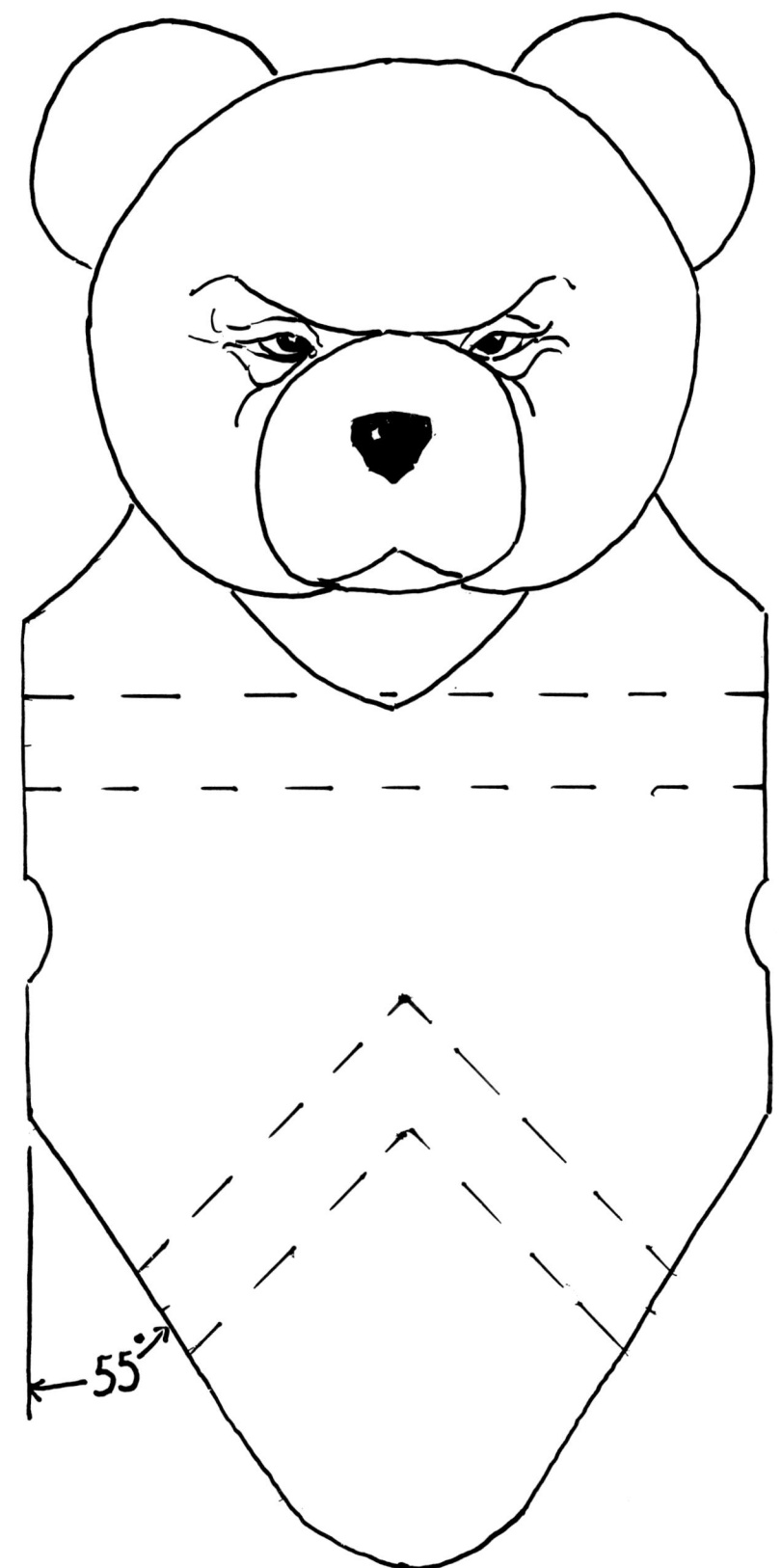

55°

# Spawning Time

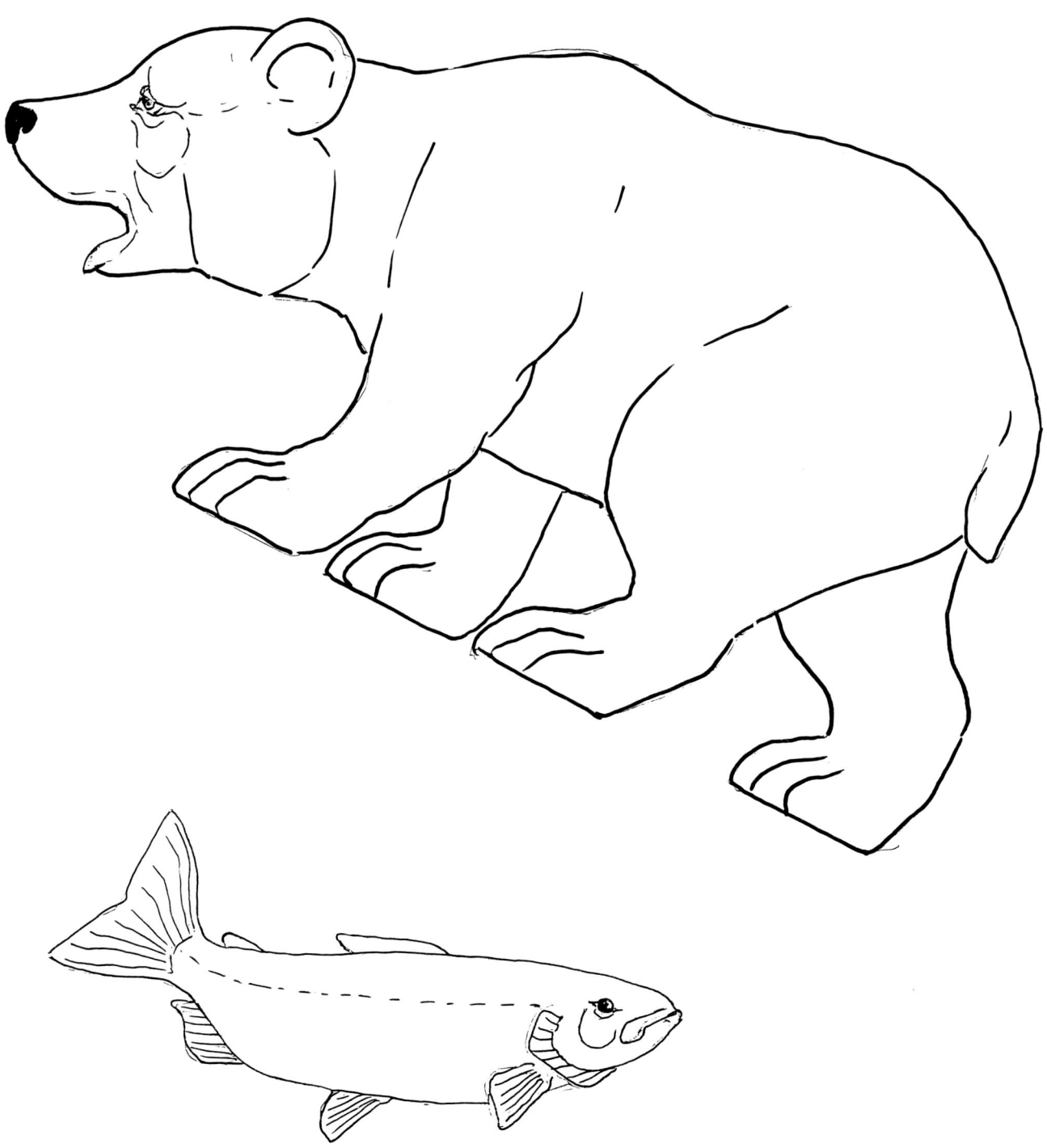

# Dancing Bare

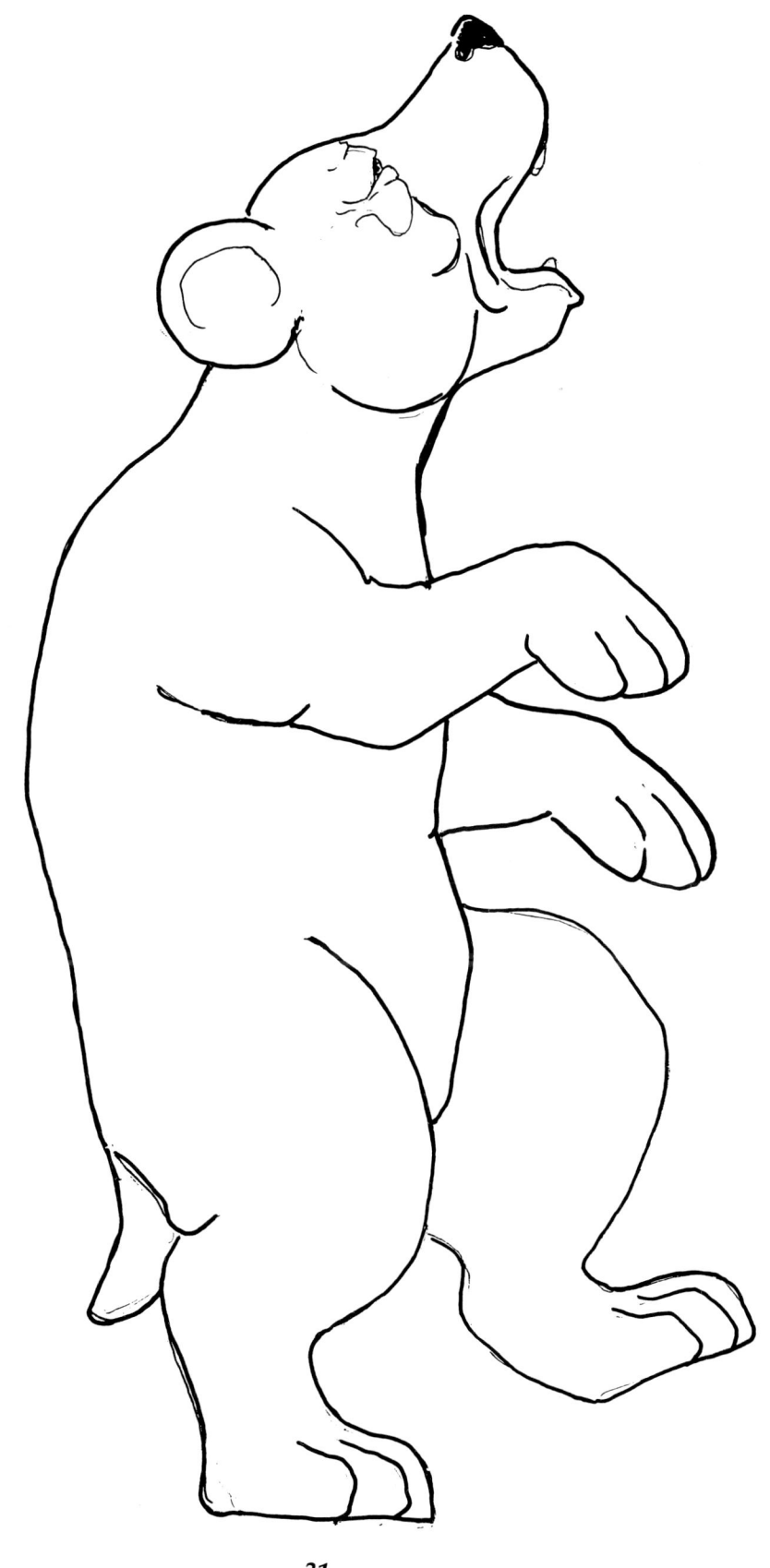

# Big Horny Hooter

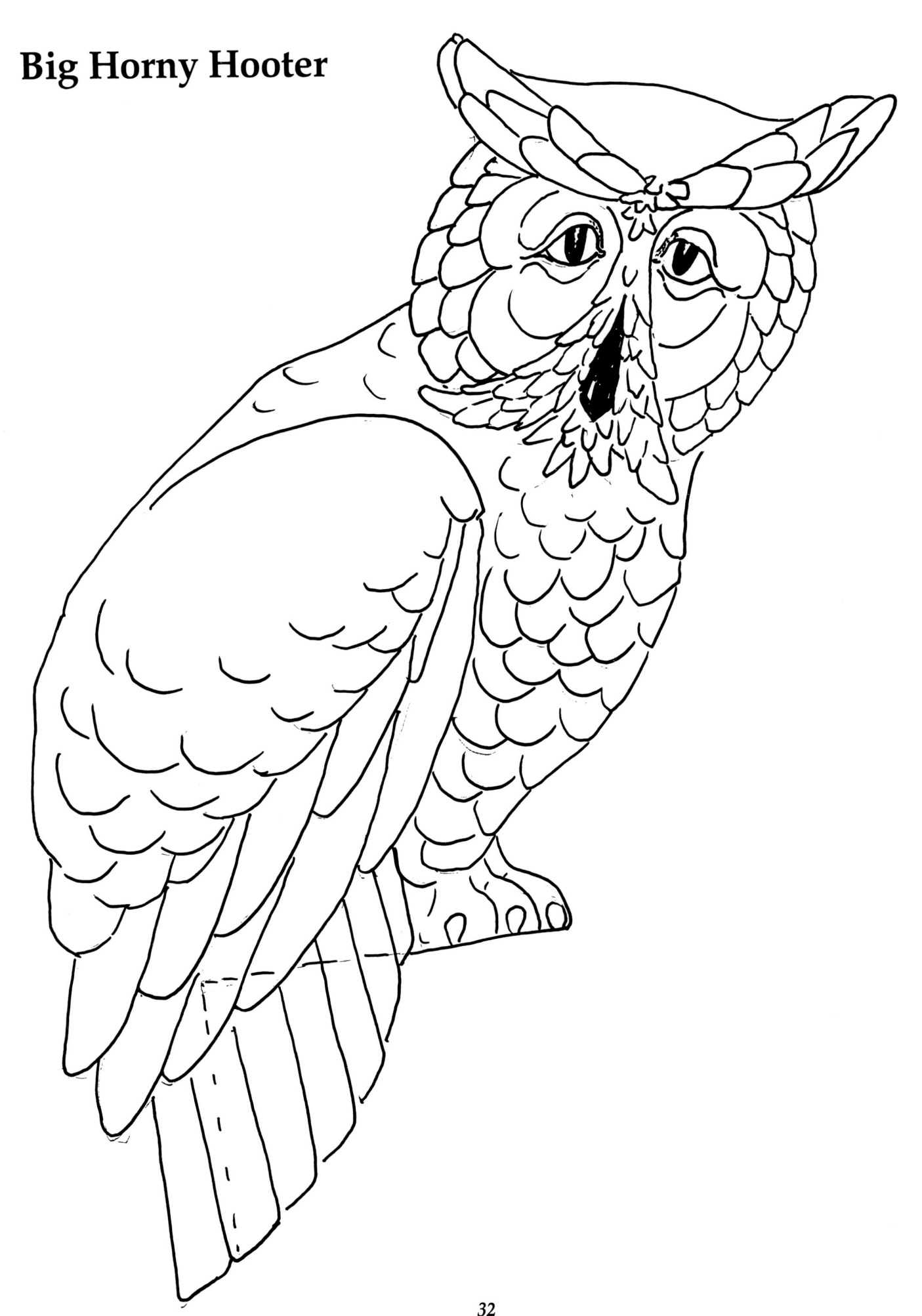

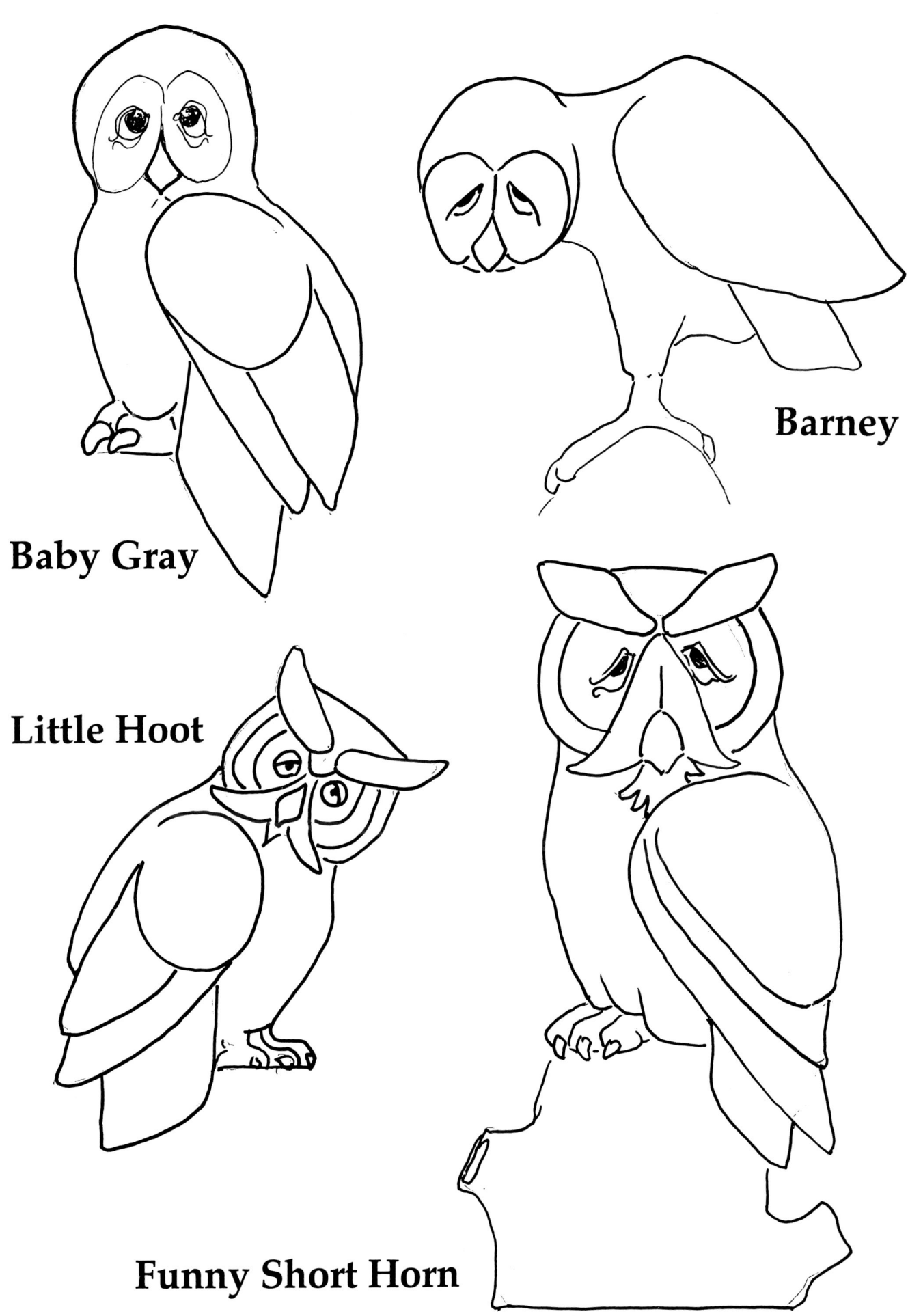

**Baby Gray**

**Barney**

**Little Hoot**

**Funny Short Horn**

# The Fawns

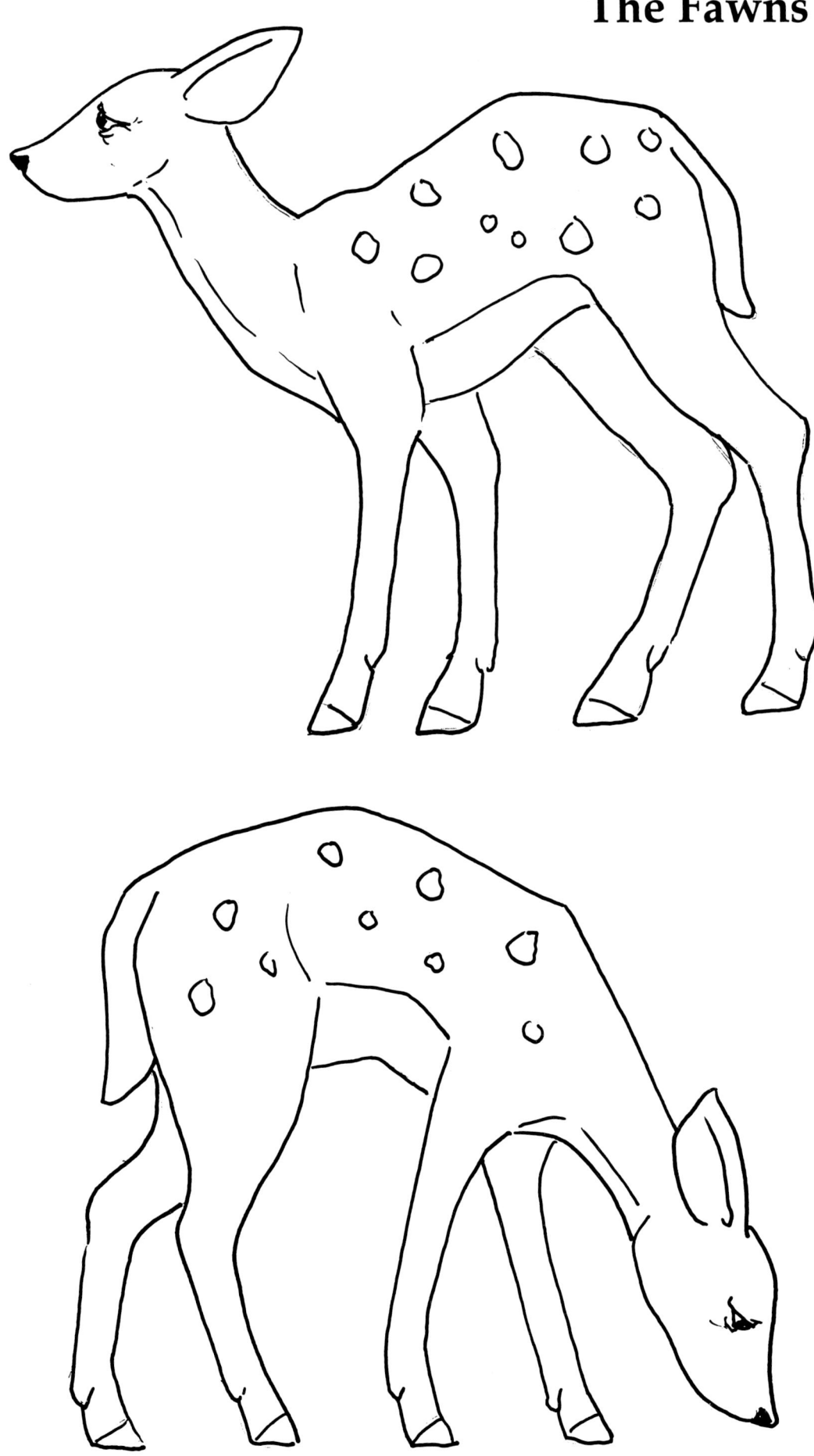

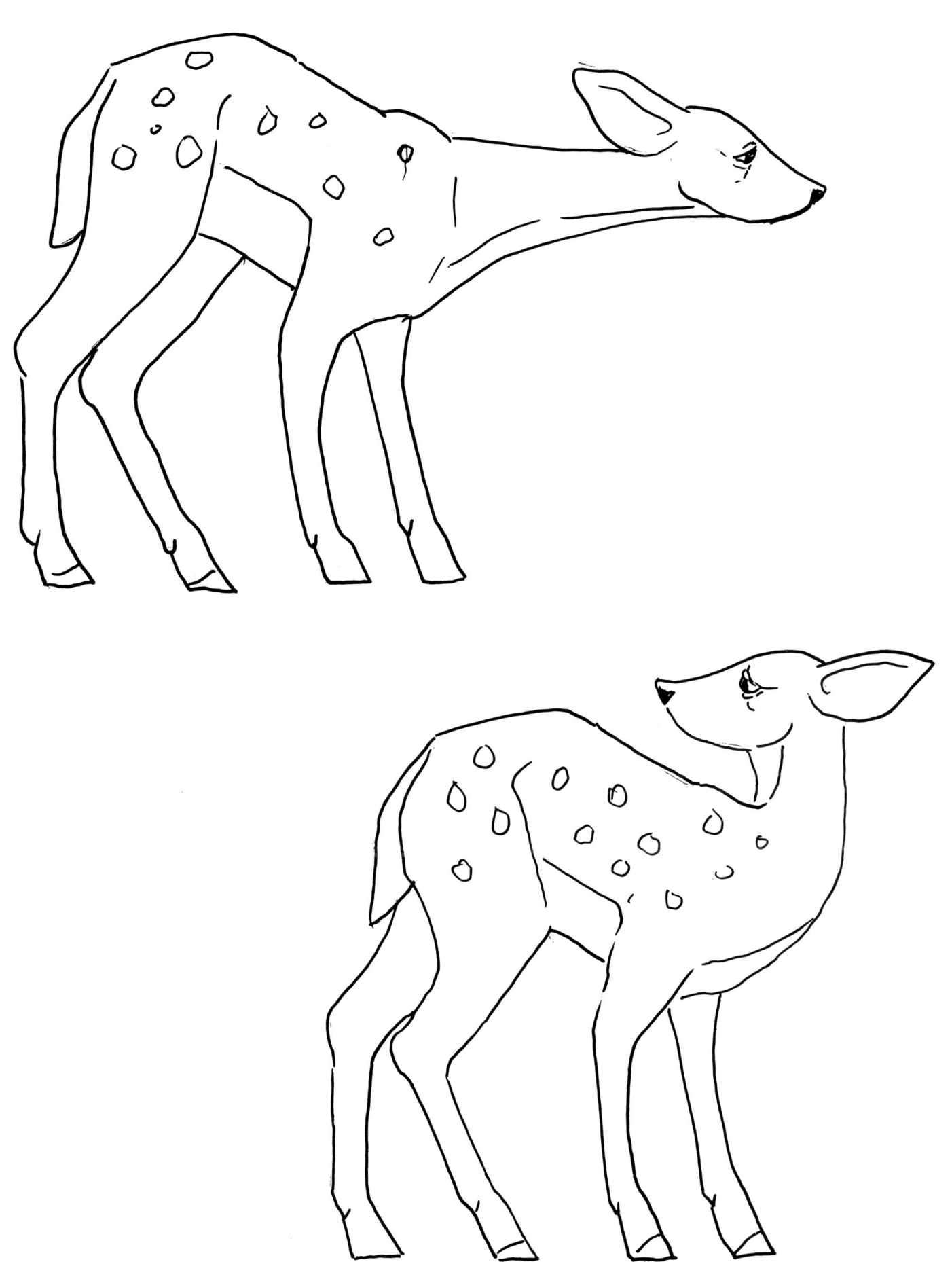

# Testing the Wind

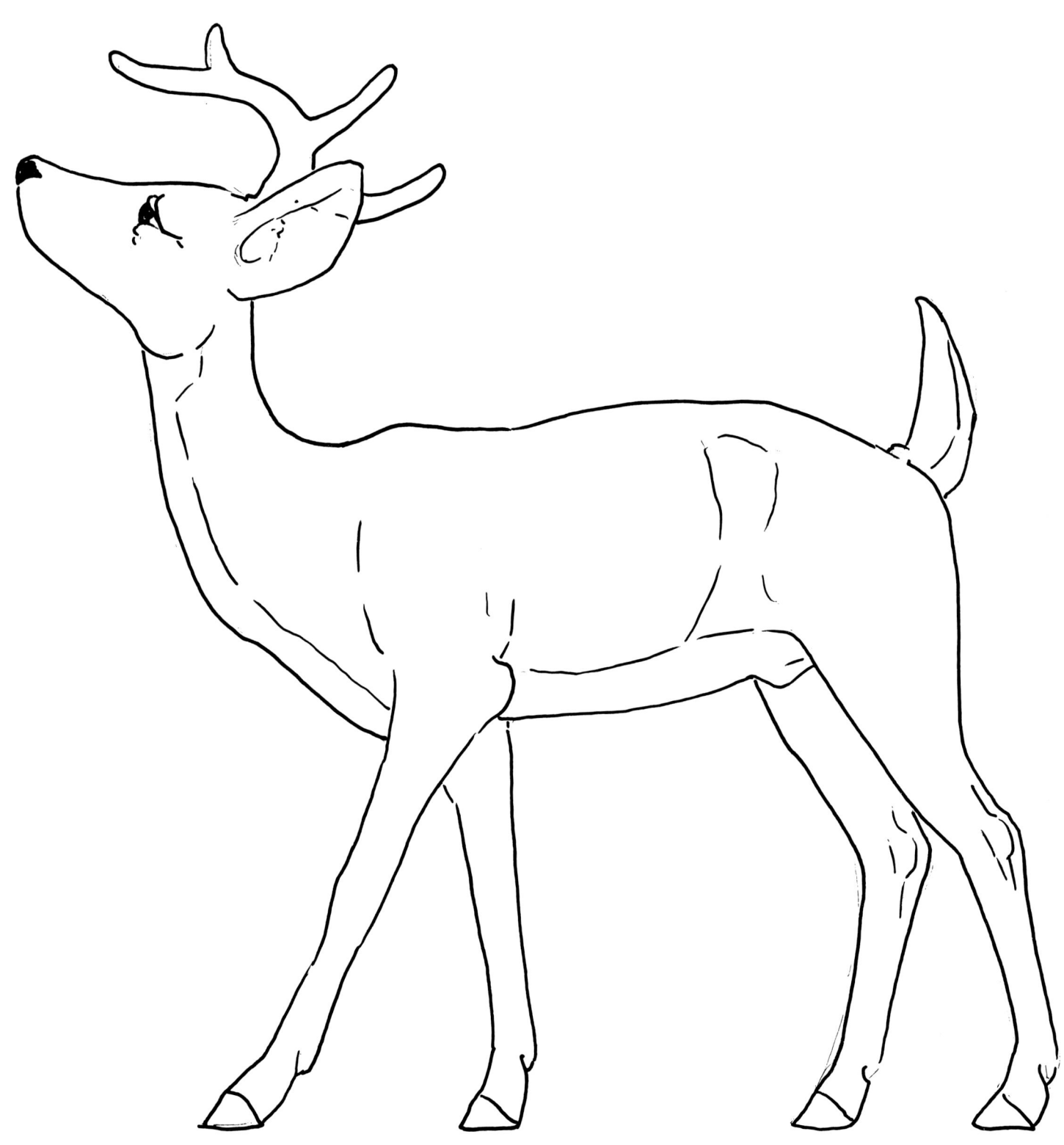

# Contented Doe

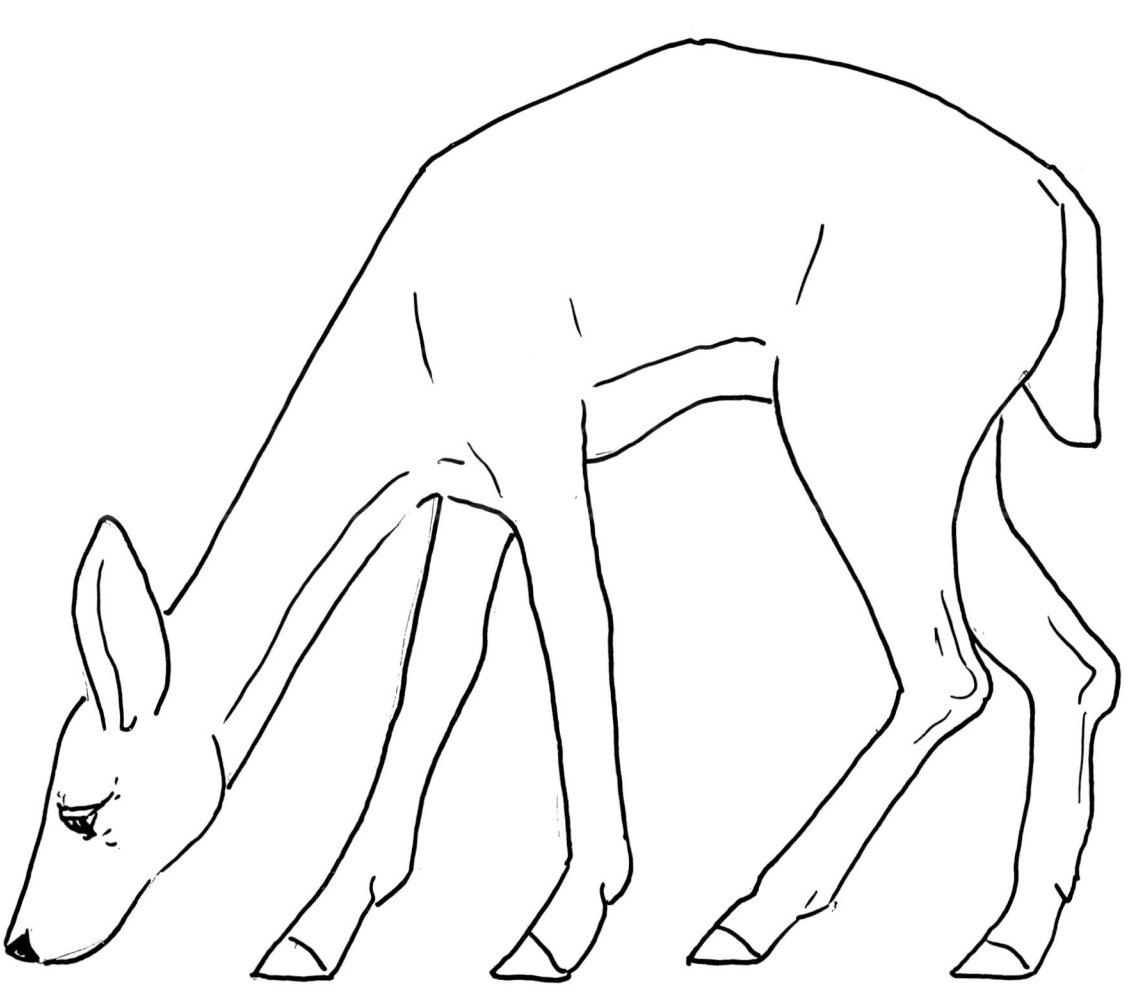

# Reindeer

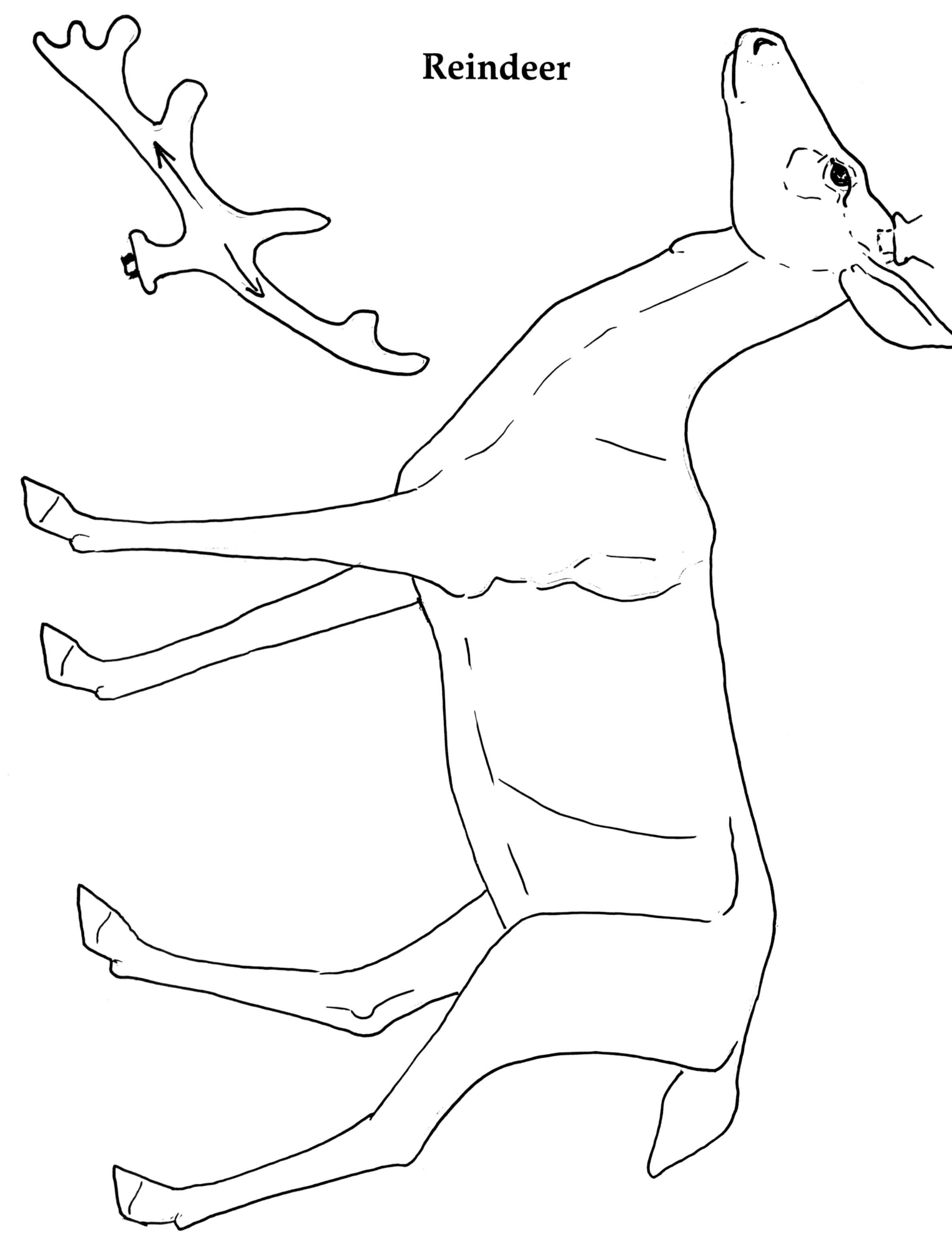

# Goats

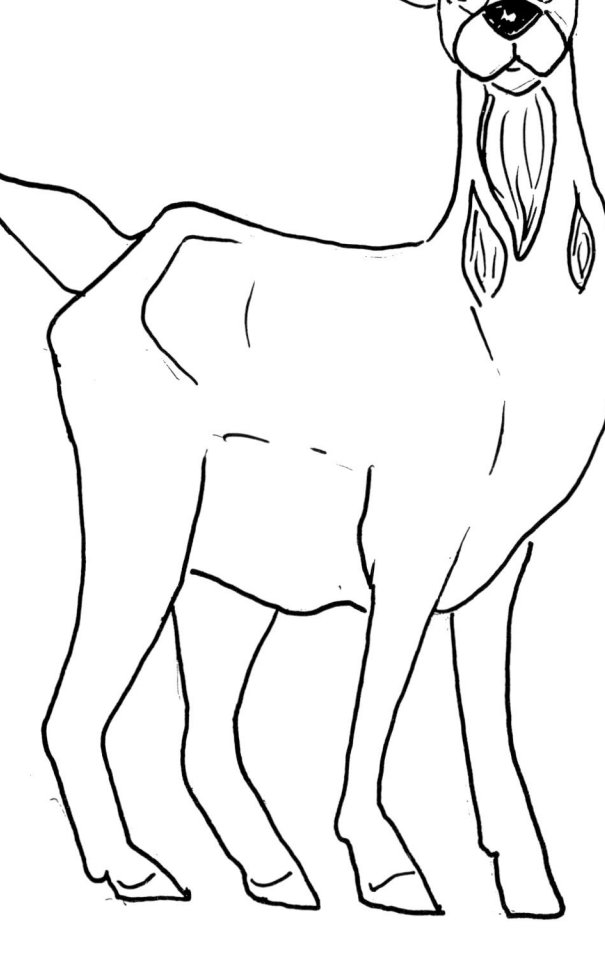

## Two Young Billies

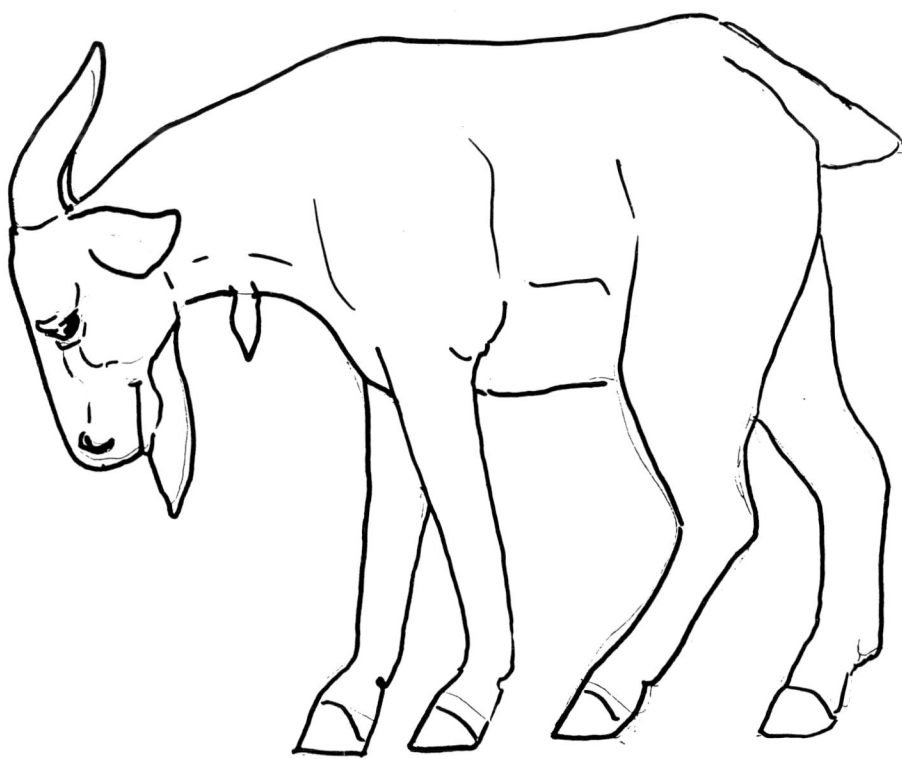

39

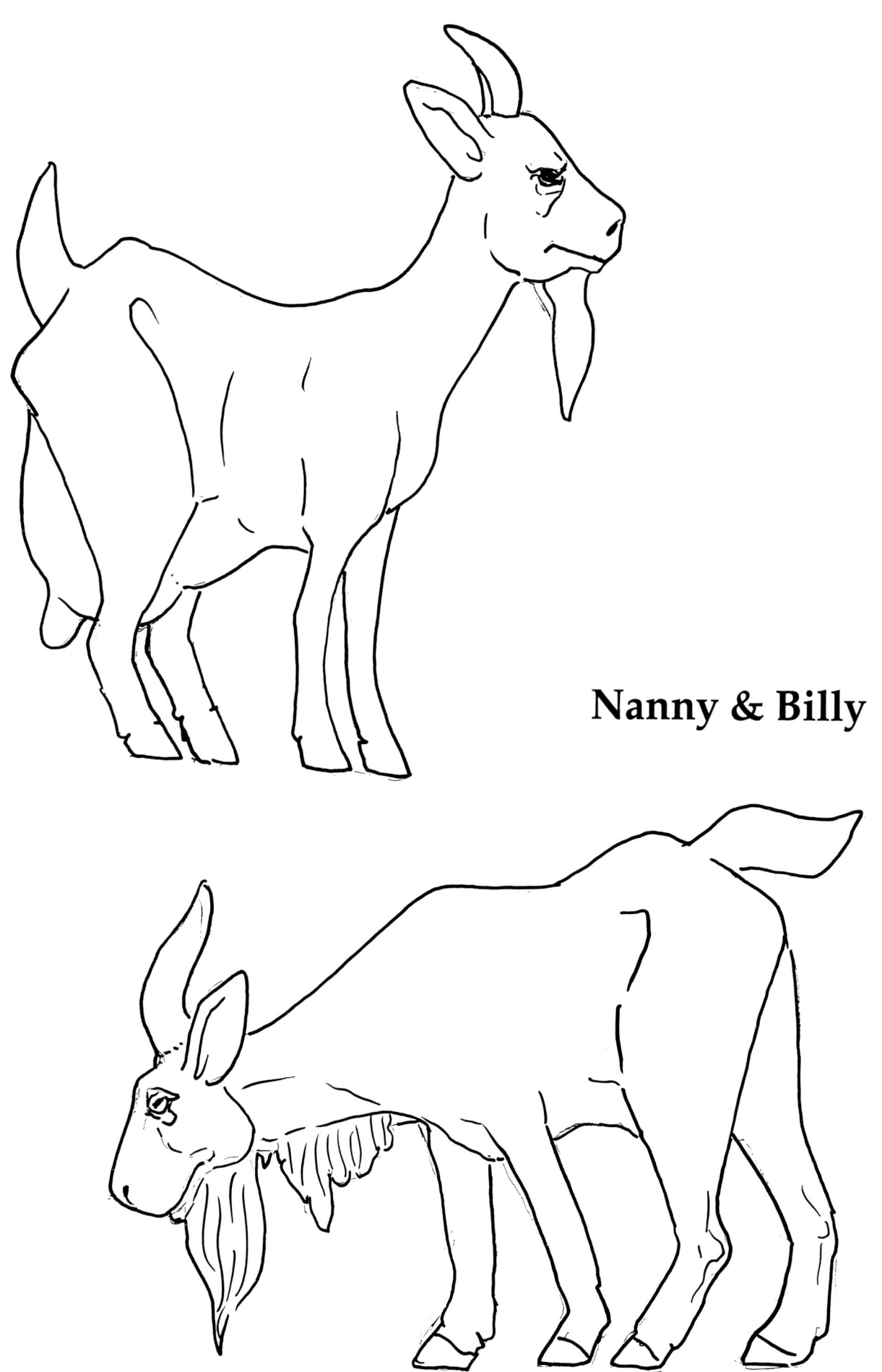

**Nanny & Billy**

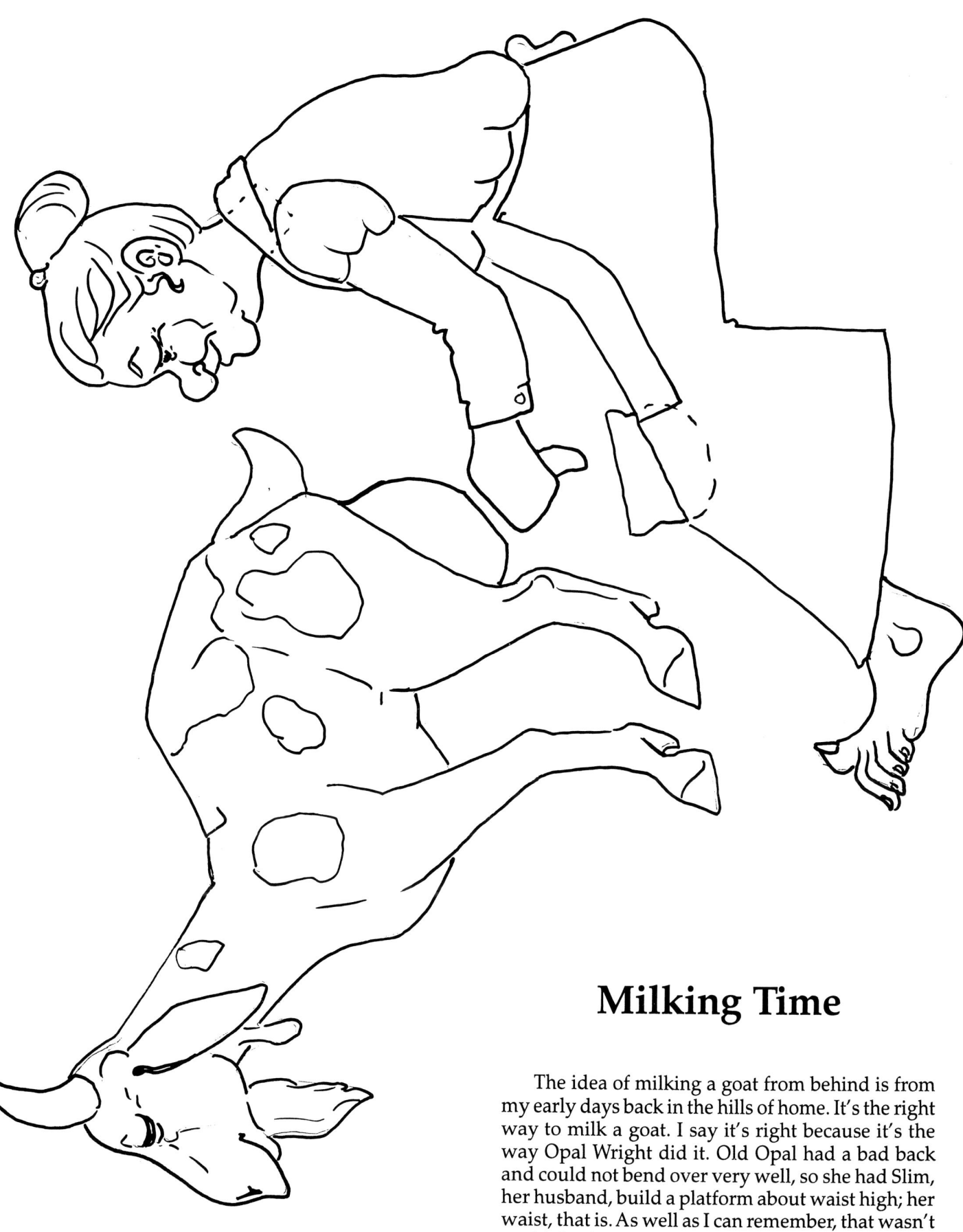

## Milking Time

The idea of milking a goat from behind is from my early days back in the hills of home. It's the right way to milk a goat. I say it's right because it's the way Opal Wright did it. Old Opal had a bad back and could not bend over very well, so she had Slim, her husband, build a platform about waist high; her waist, that is. As well as I can remember, that wasn't too high. That way she could walk up and milk them from behind. By the way, the goats were well trained and knew darn well not to get anything in the pail but milk.

41

# Smilin' Jack

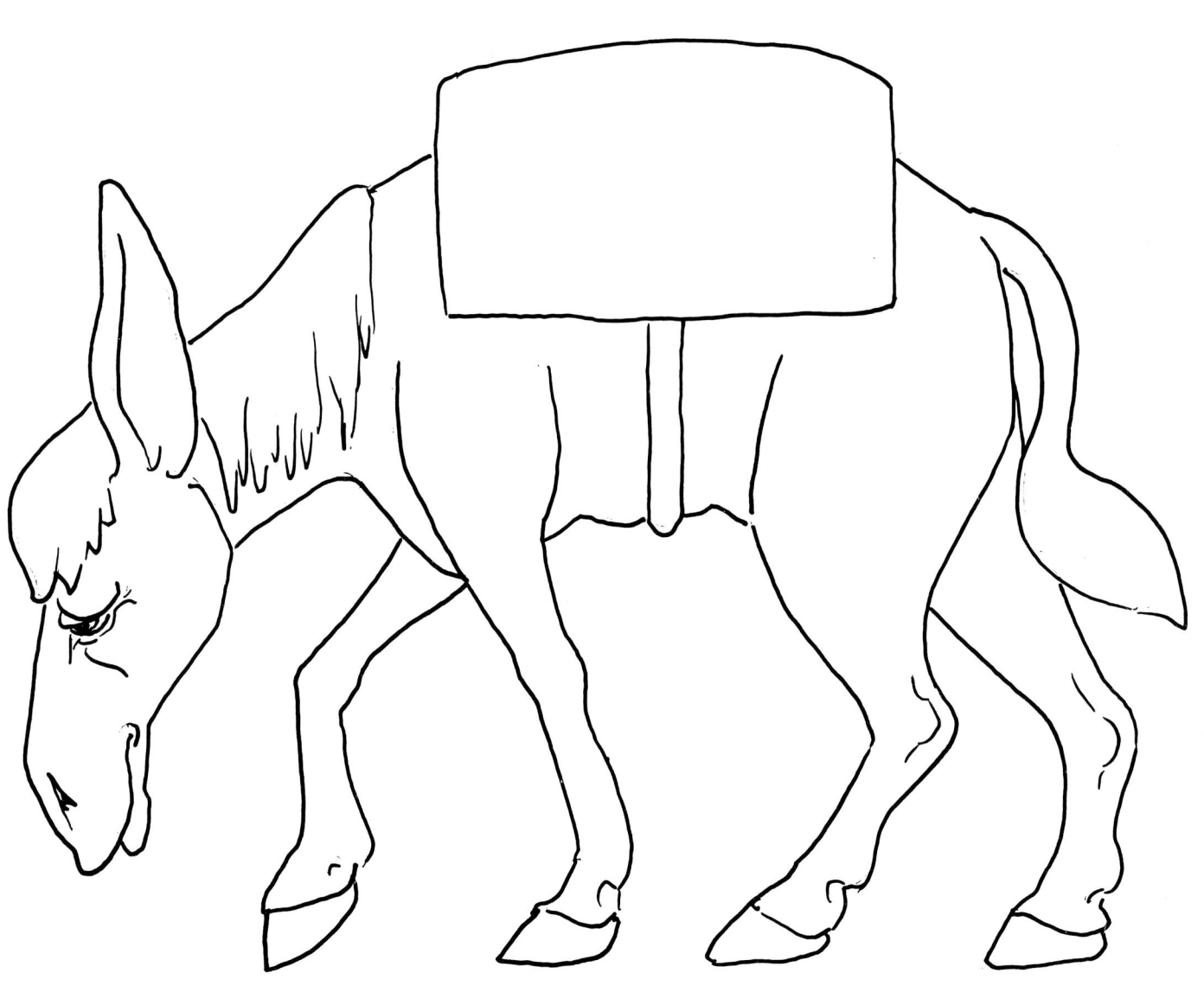

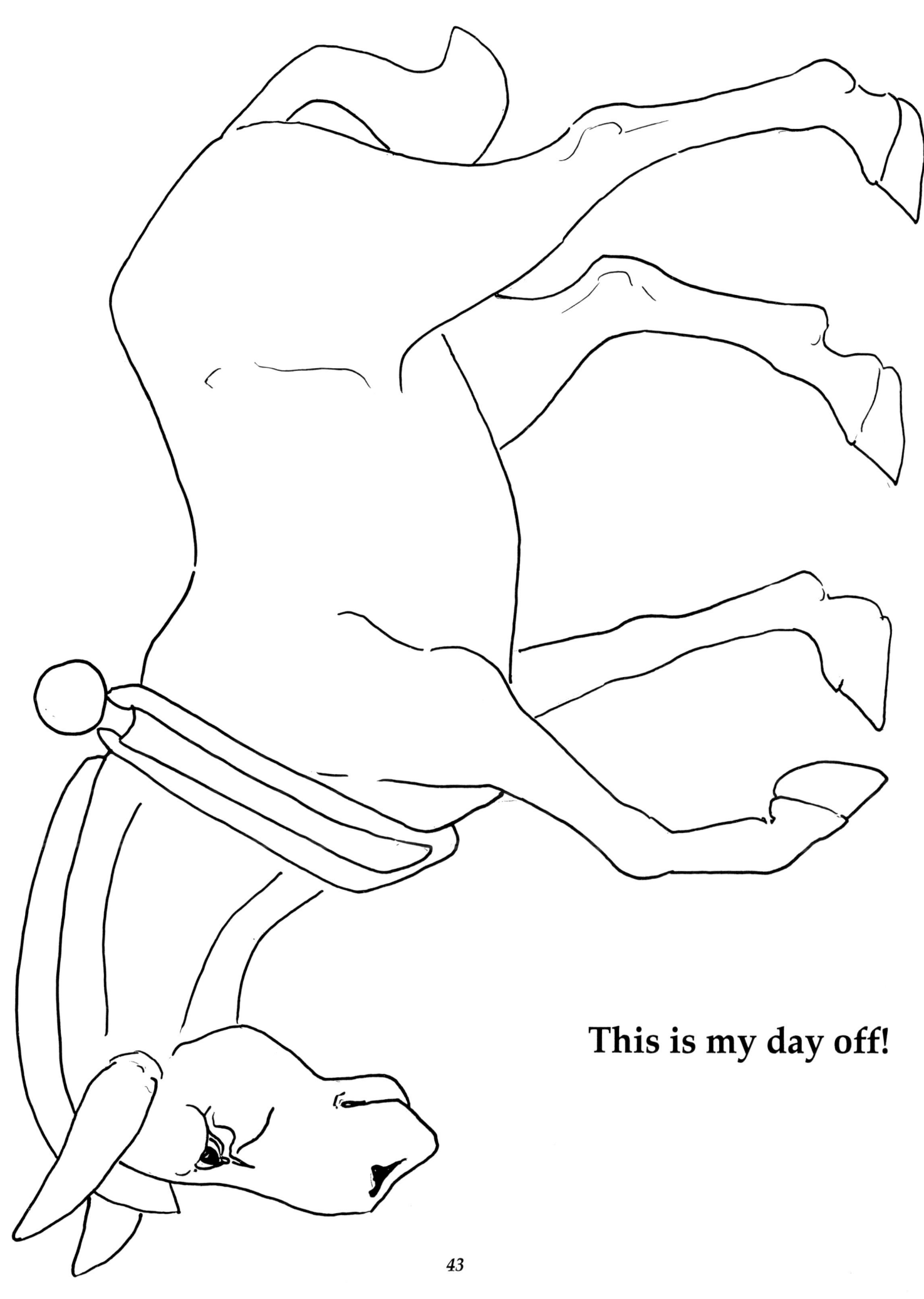

This is my day off!

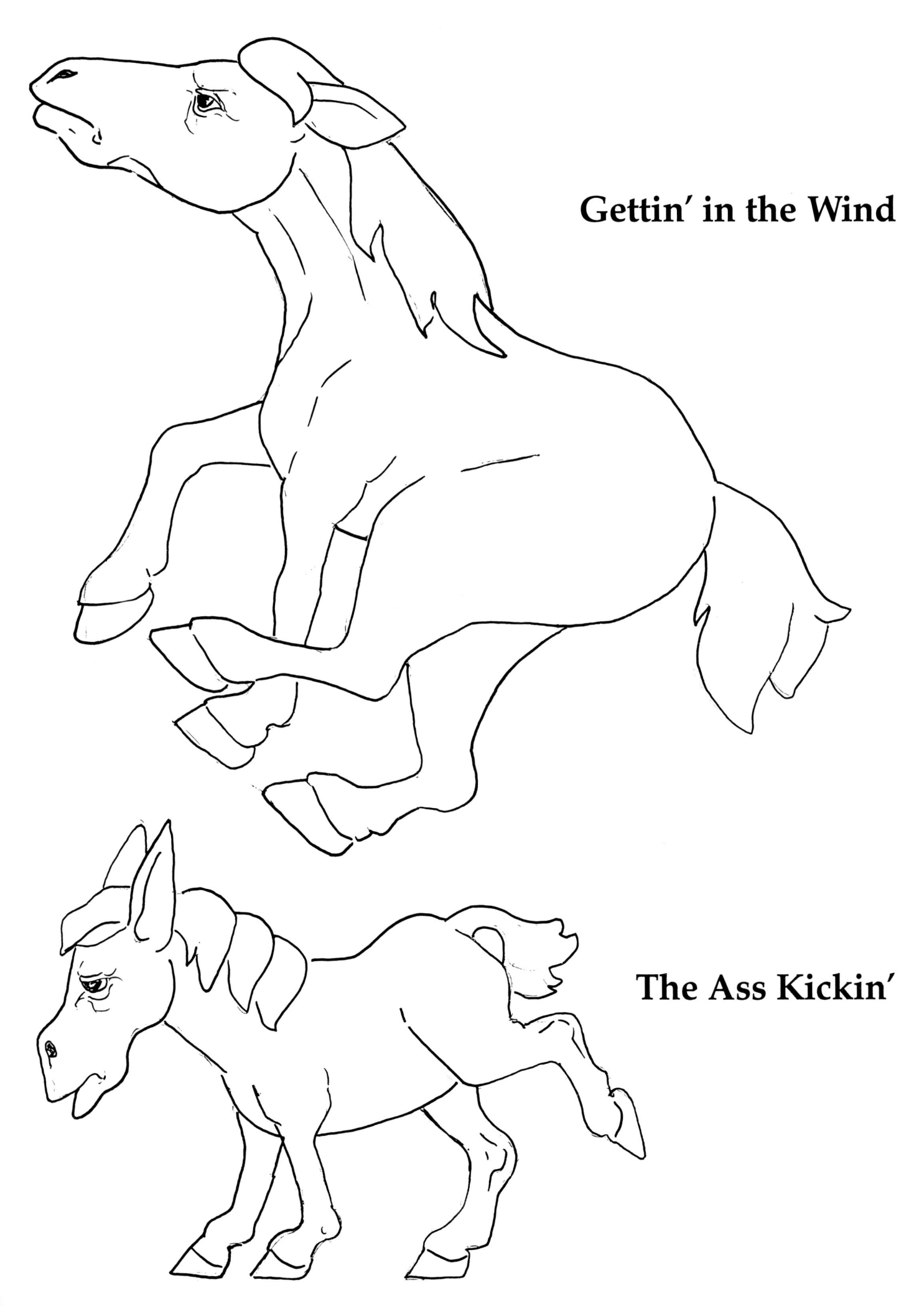

Gettin' in the Wind

The Ass Kickin'

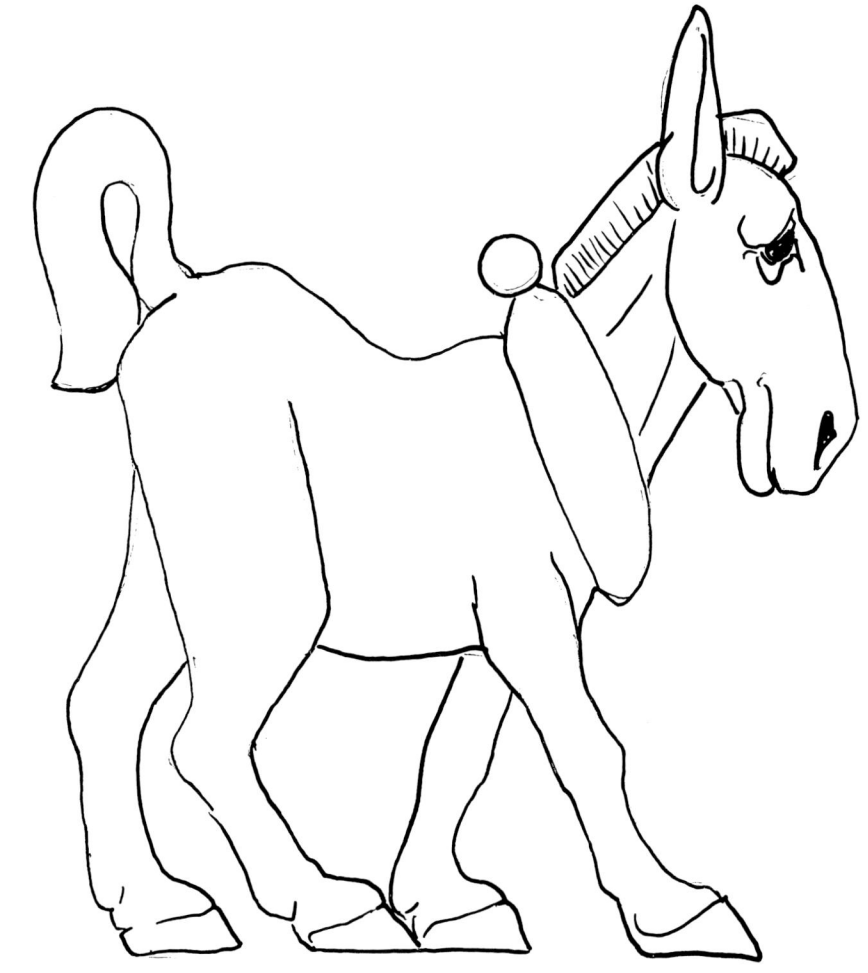

## Workin' Pair

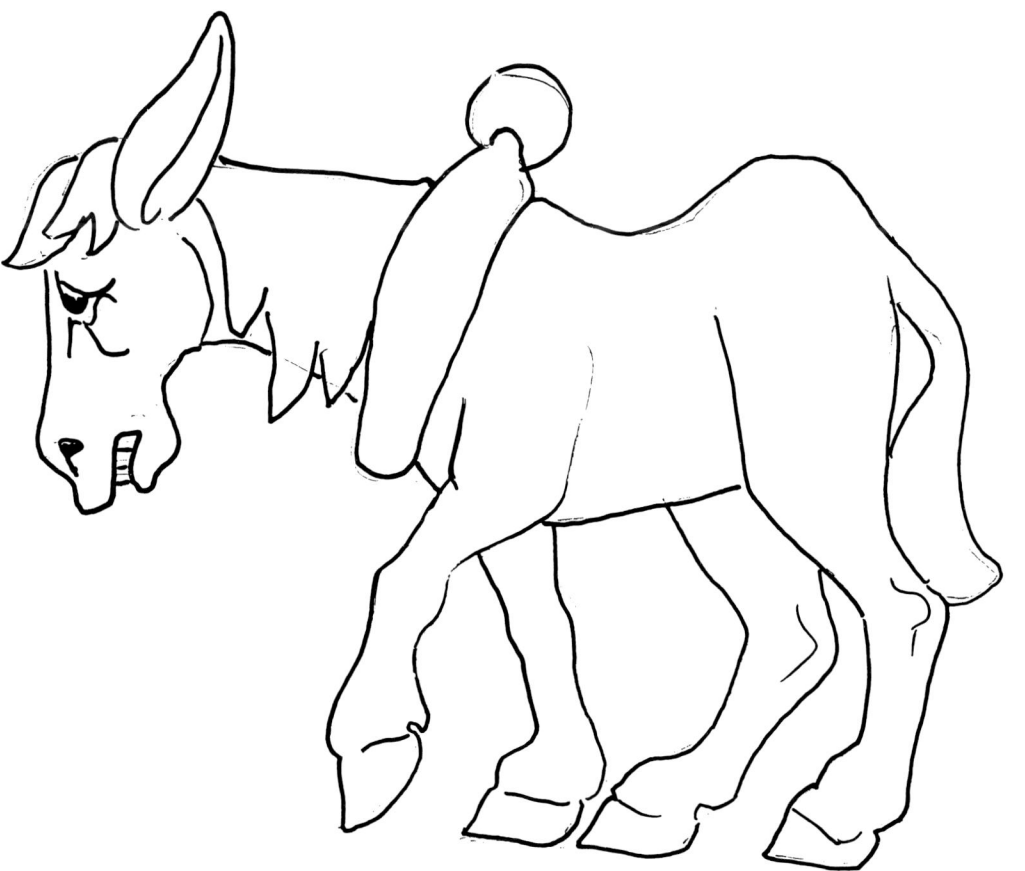

45

# Too Much
# Horsin' Around

# Udderly Marvelous Maize, or 4 on the Floor

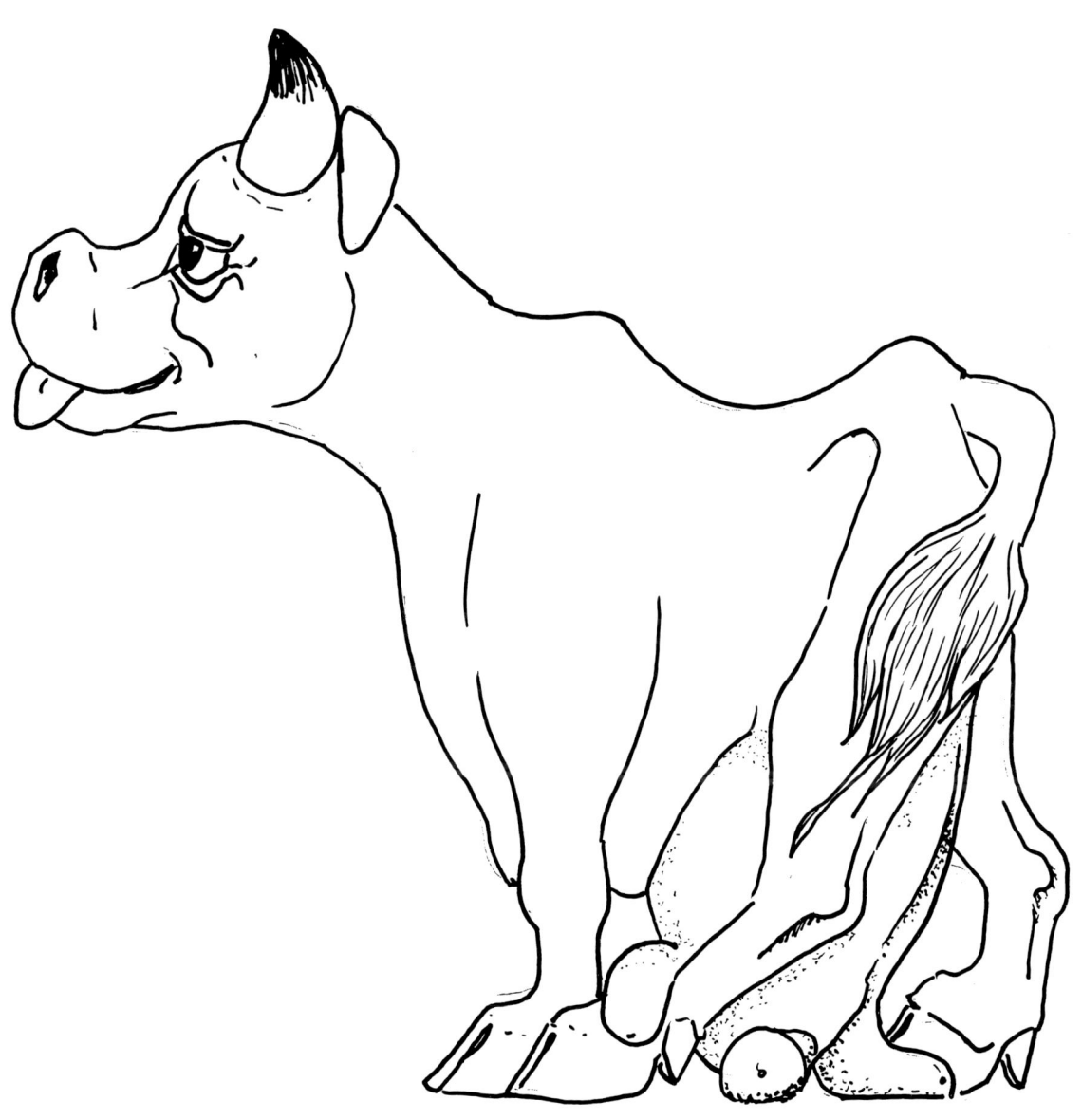

# The Divine Bovines

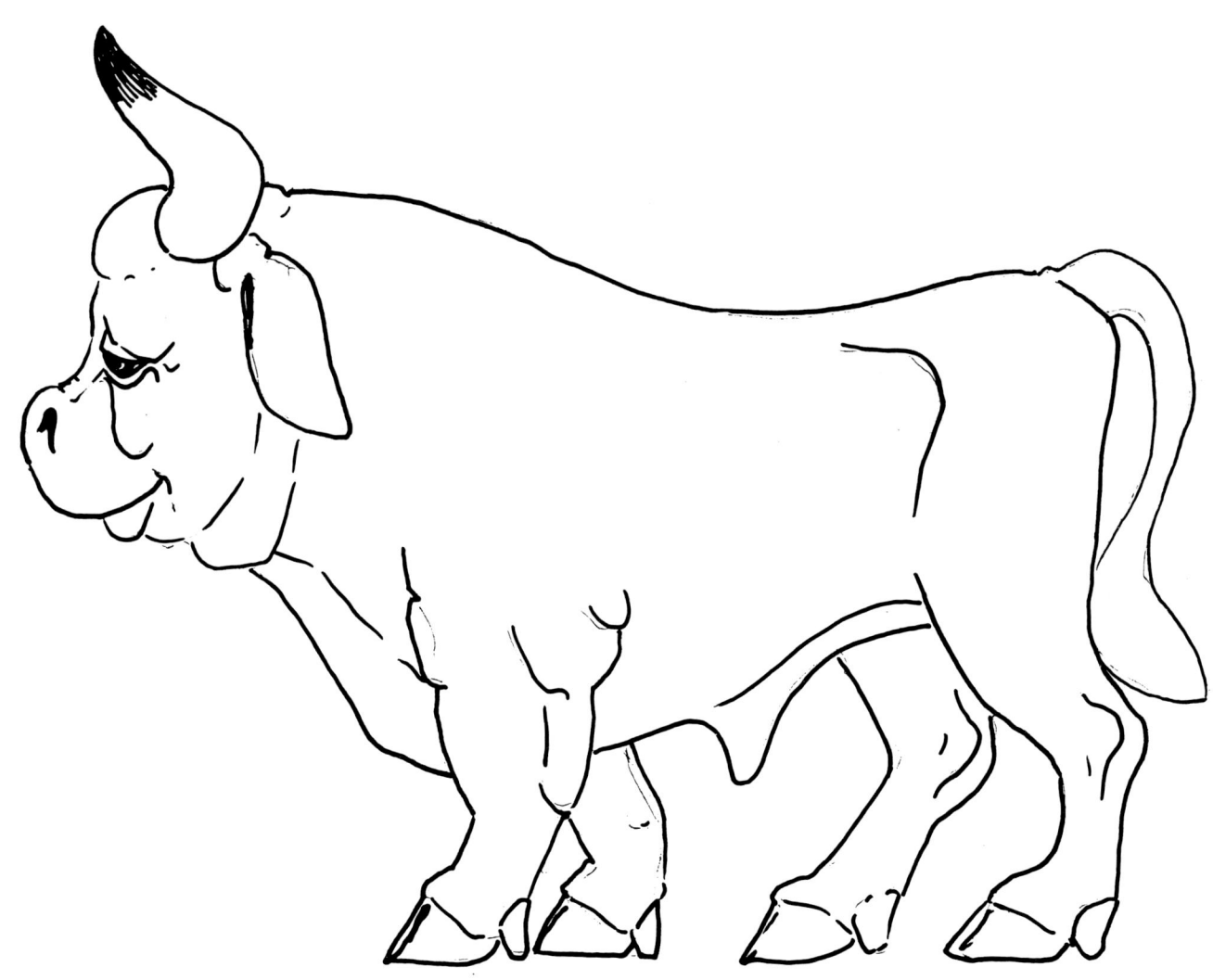

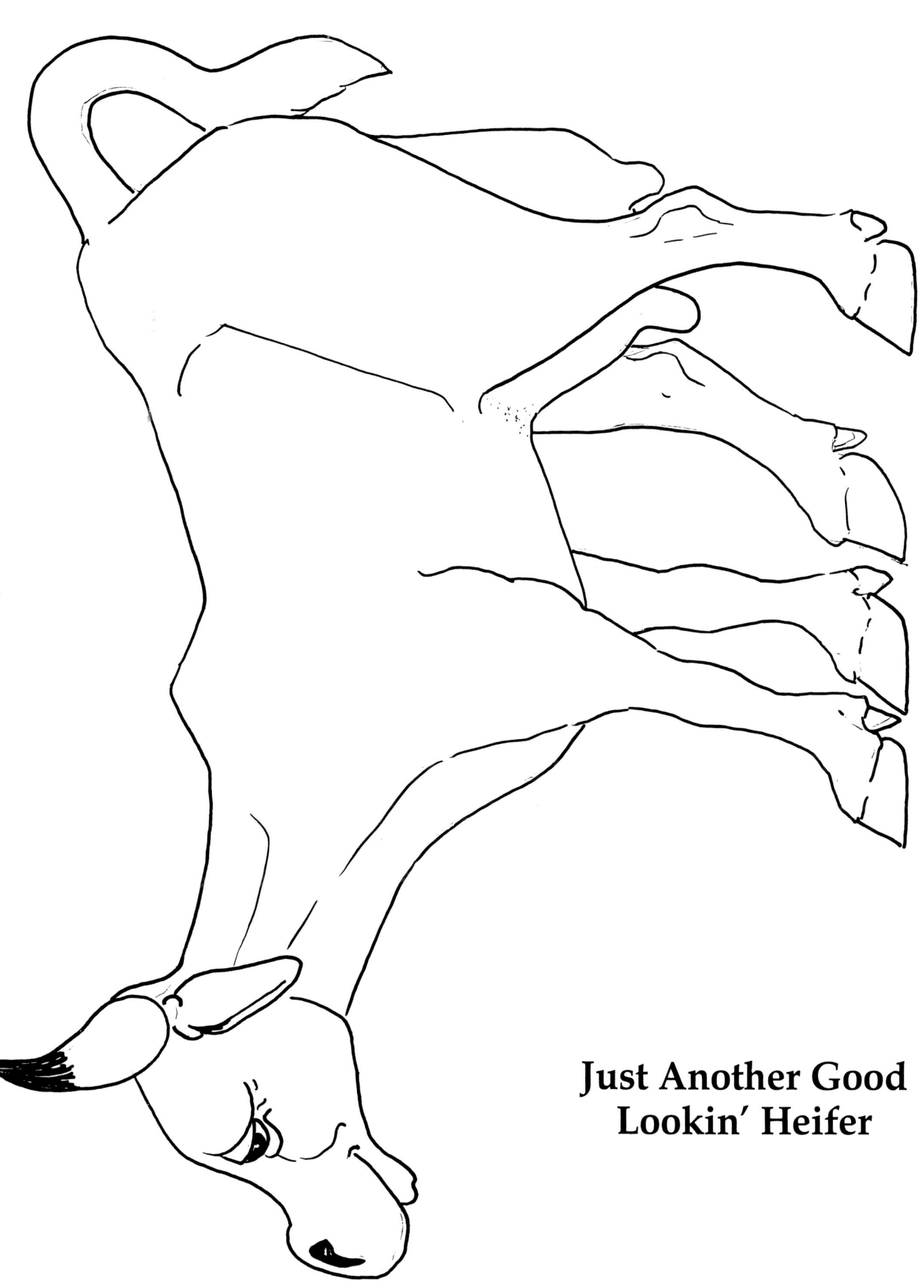

**Just Another Good Lookin' Heifer**

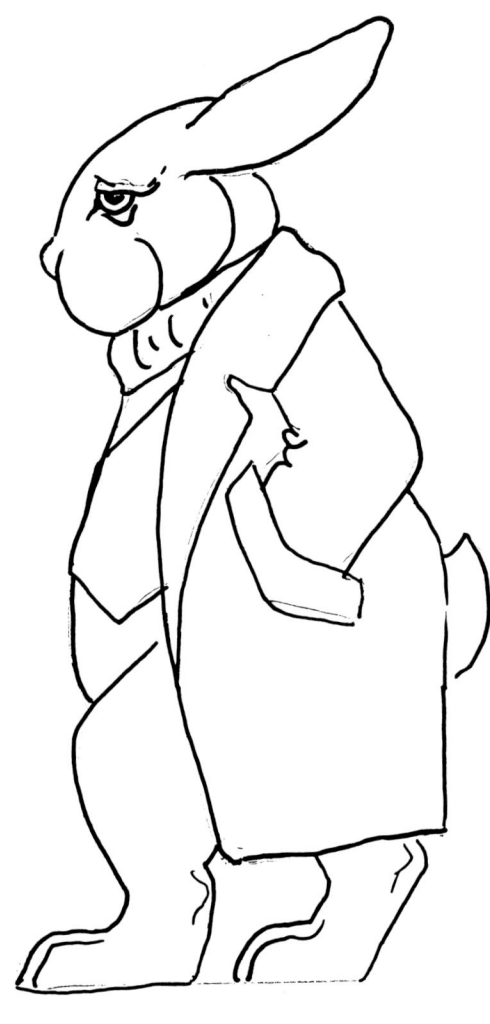

**Papa**

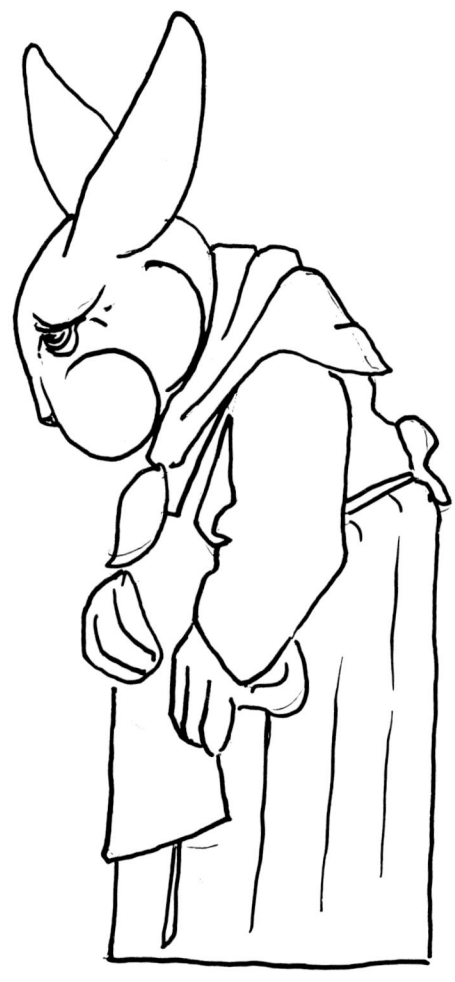

**Mama**

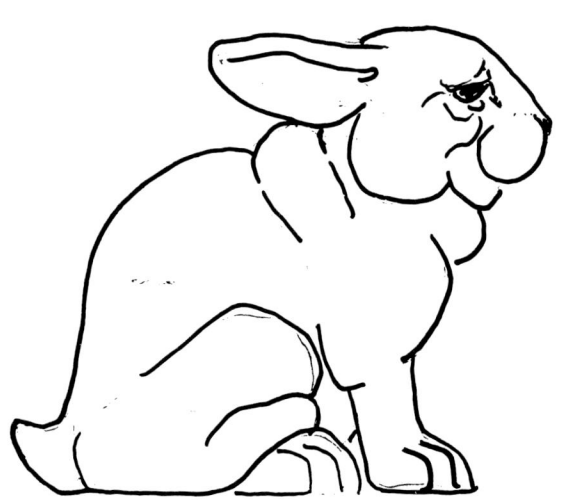

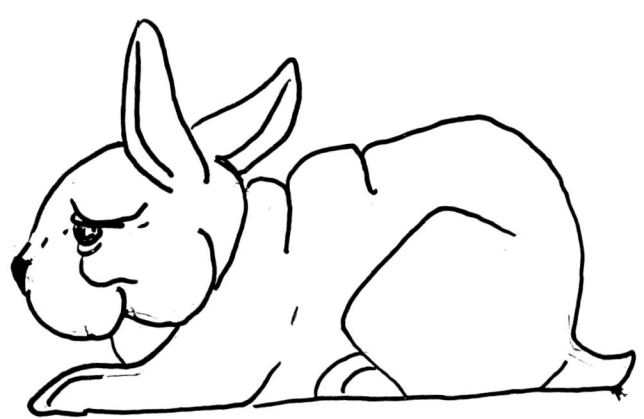

**Two Funny Bunnies**

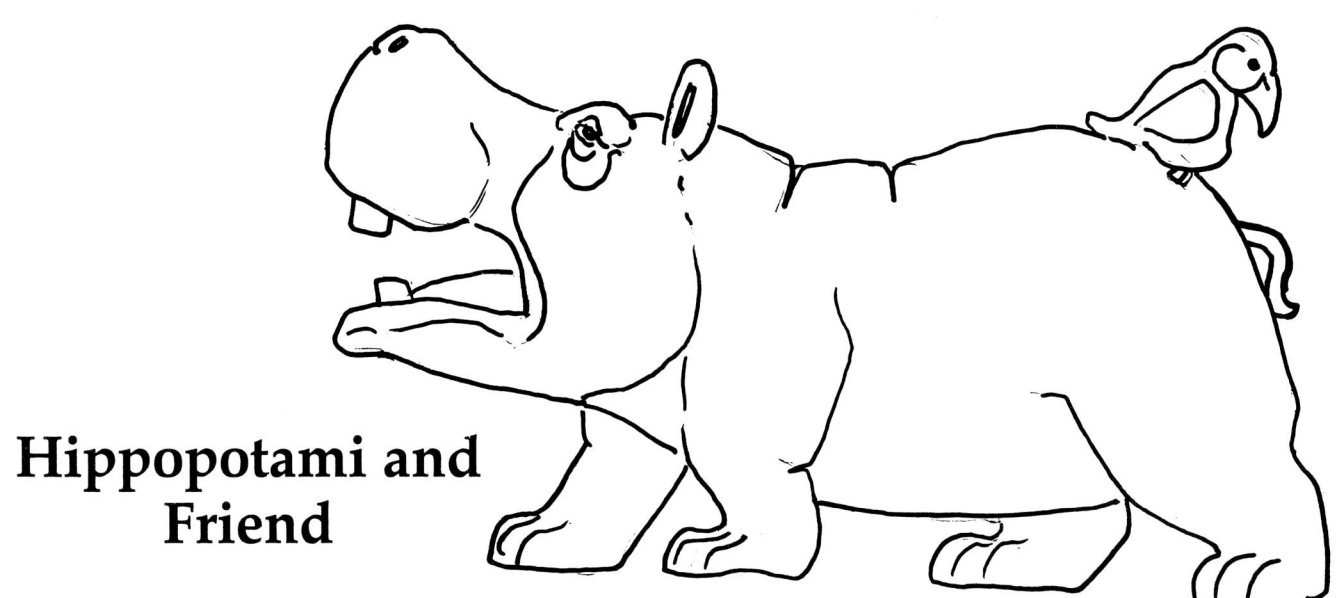

# Hippopotami and Friend

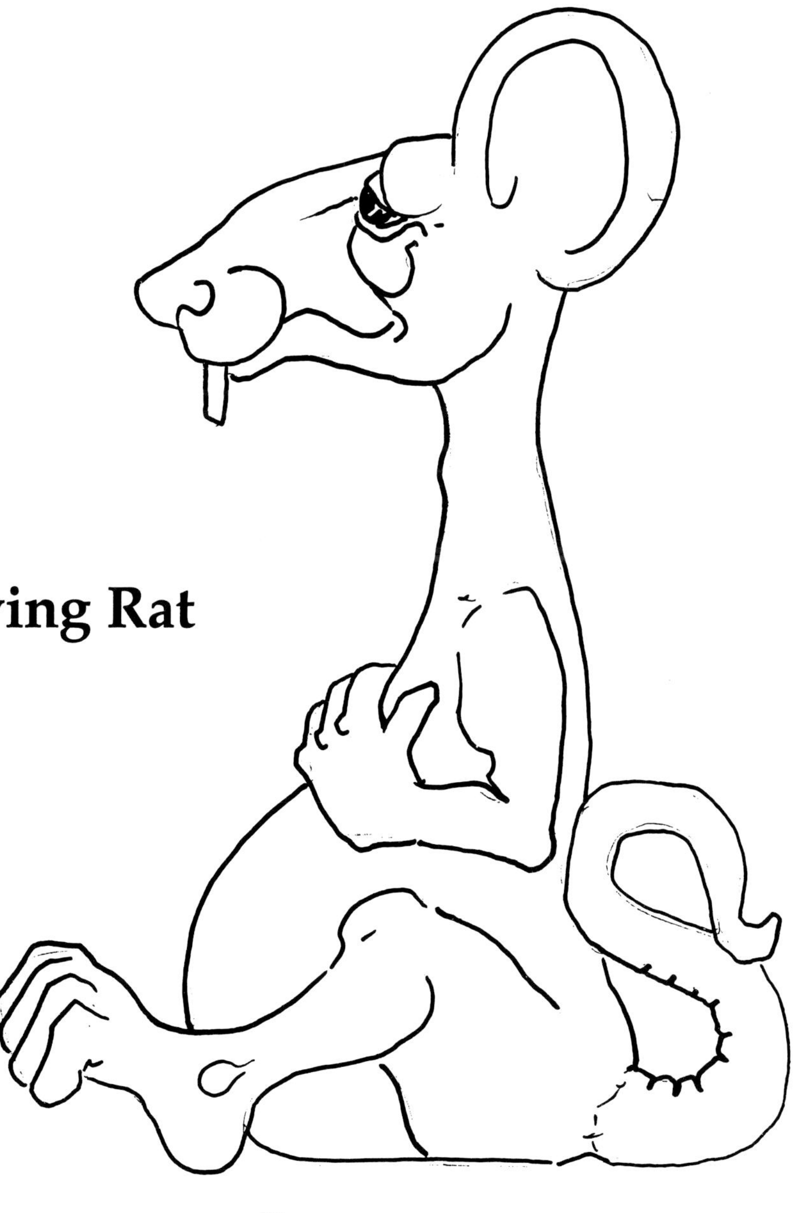

# The Card Carrying Rat

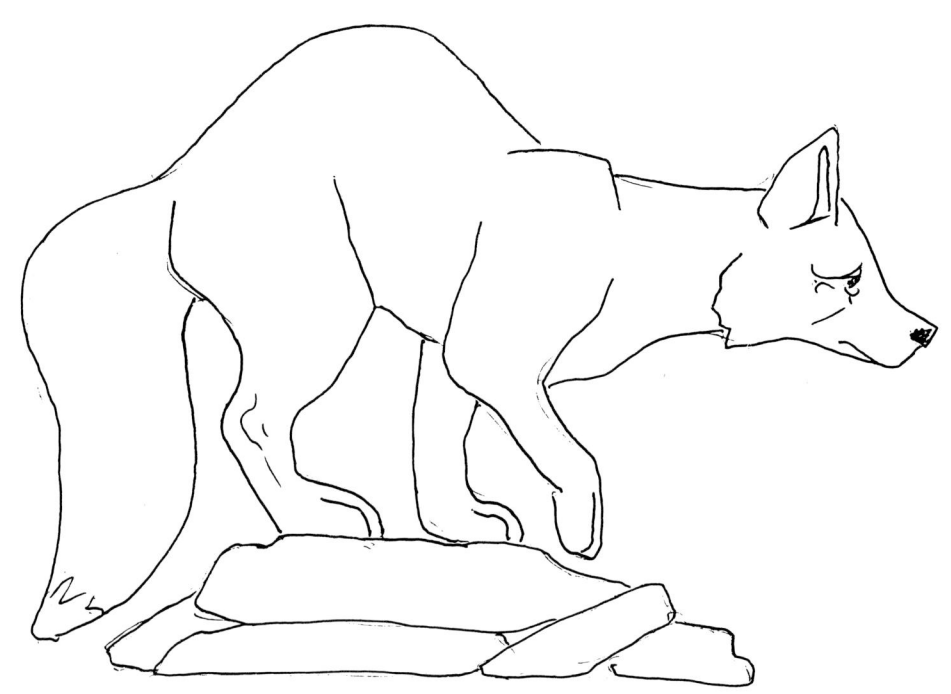

**Sly Renard the Fox**

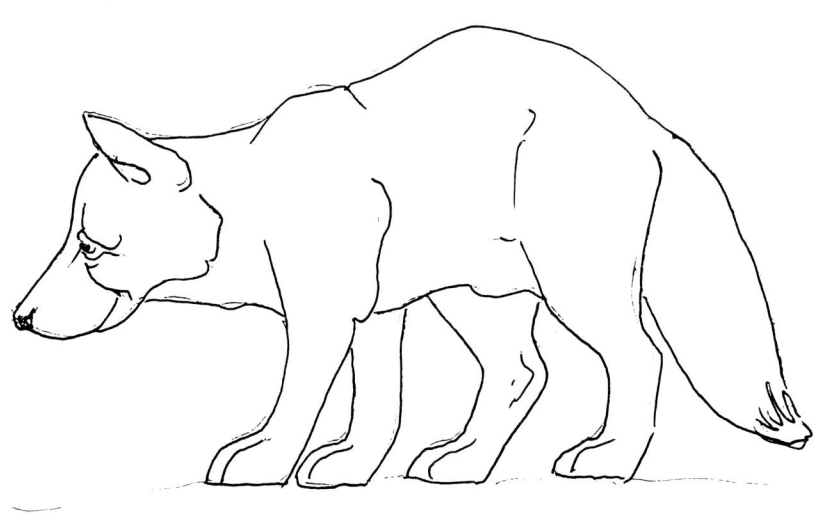

**Mr. Good Guy**

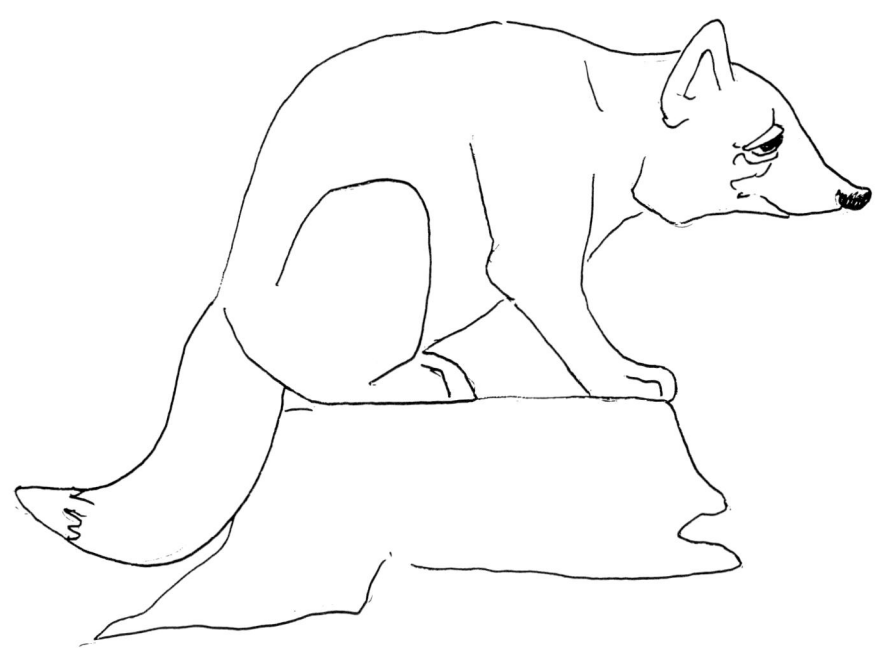

# The Rabbit Got Away

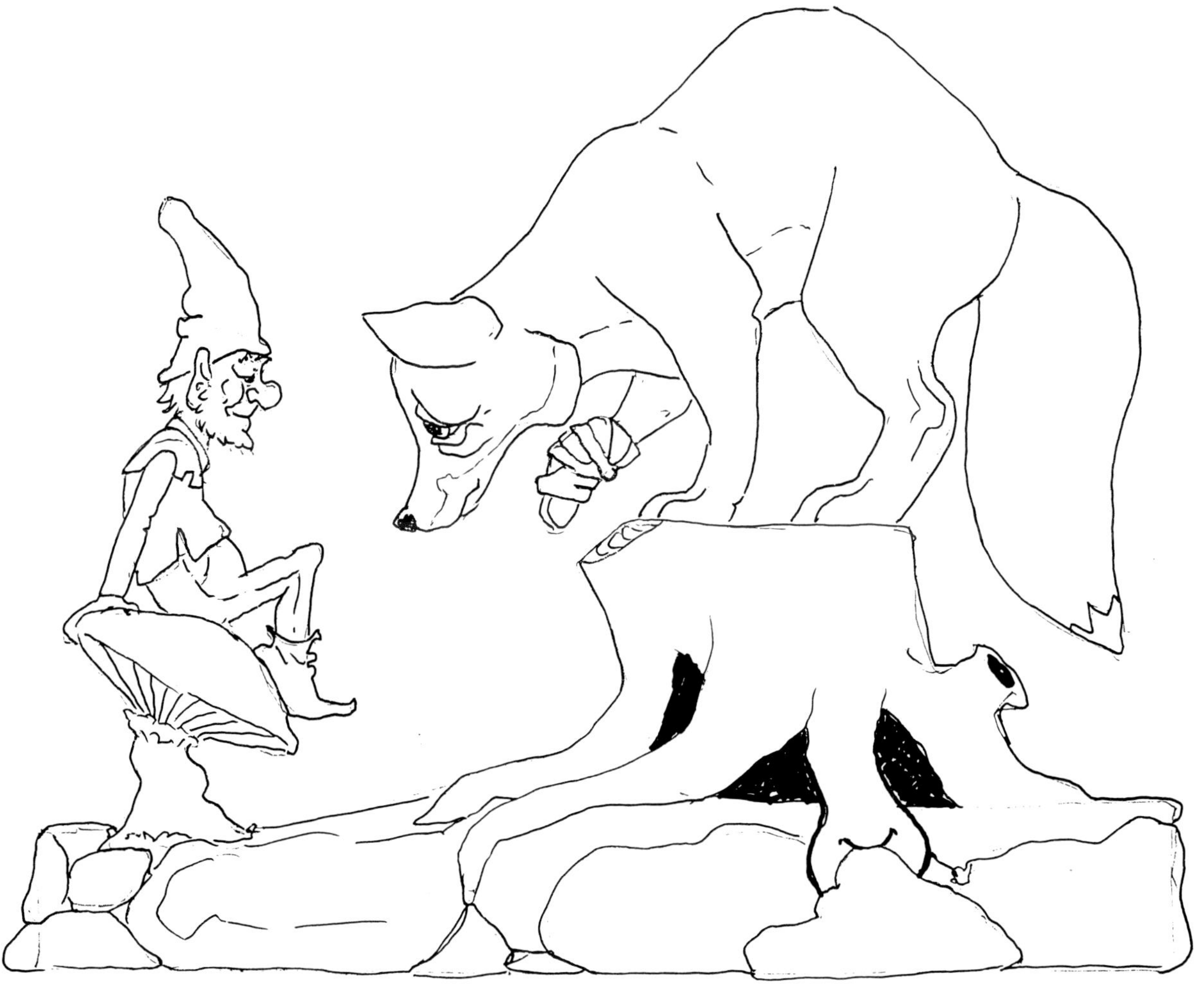

# Going to the Healer for Help

# Fox Squirrel

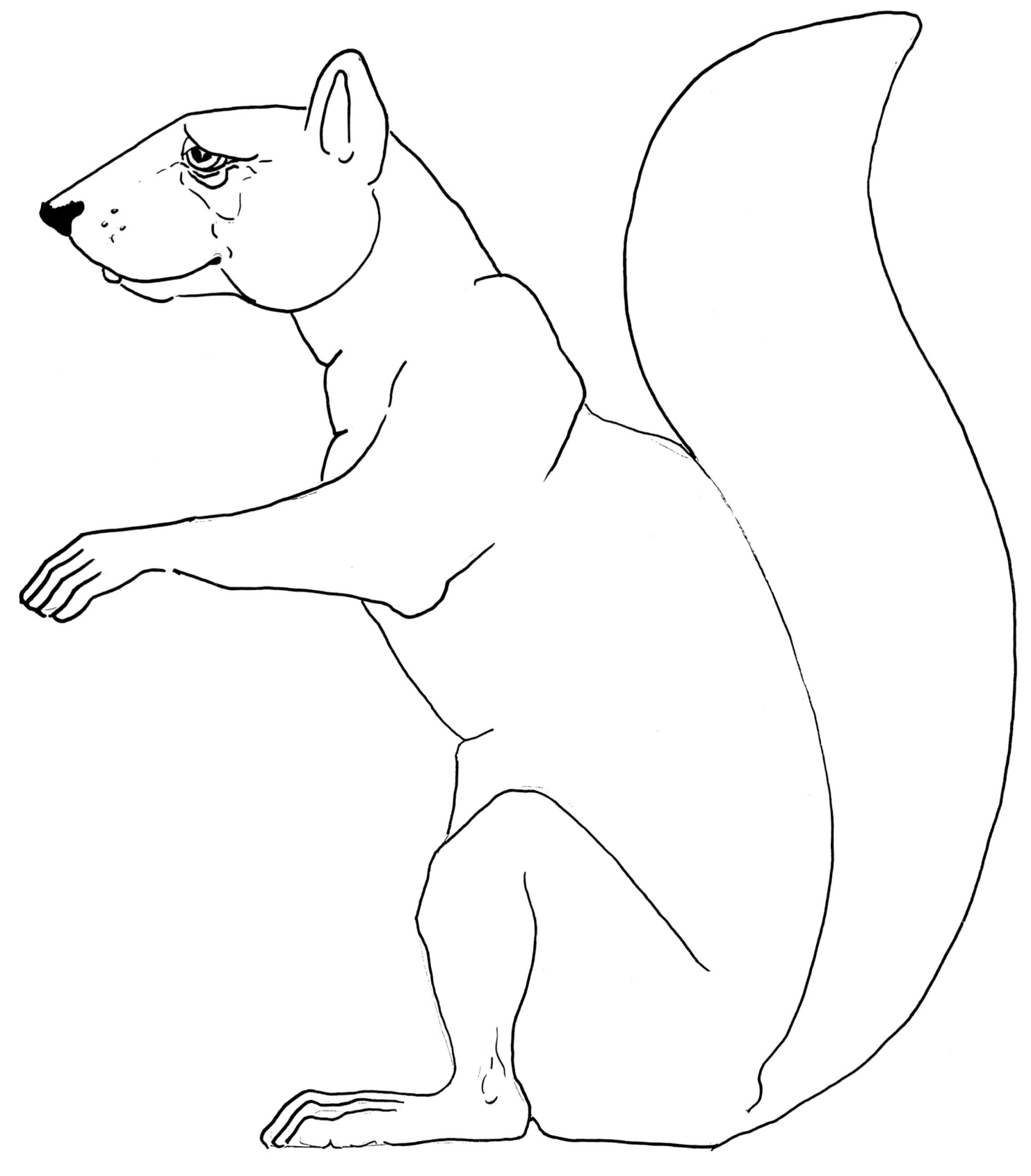

# Buffalo

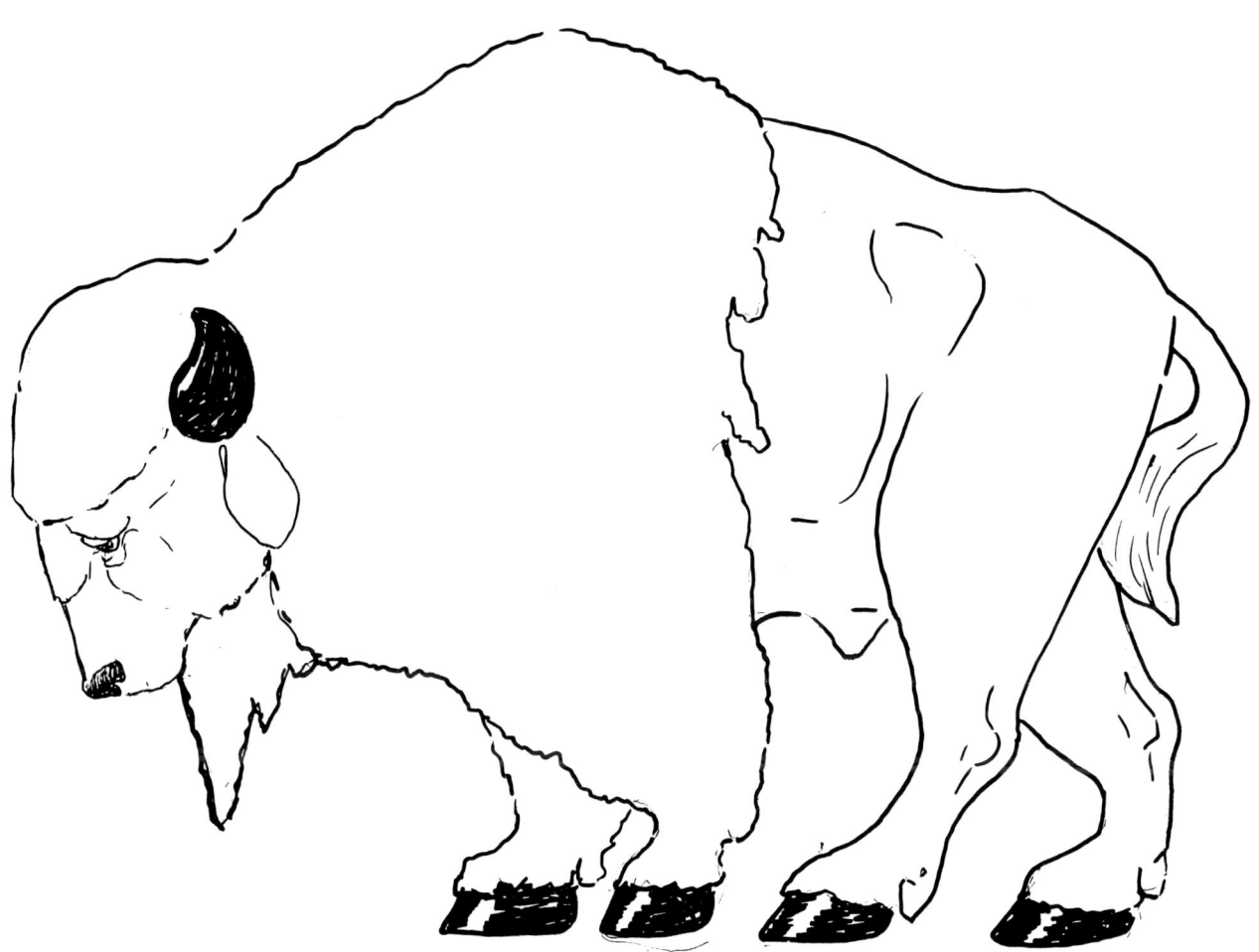

# The King

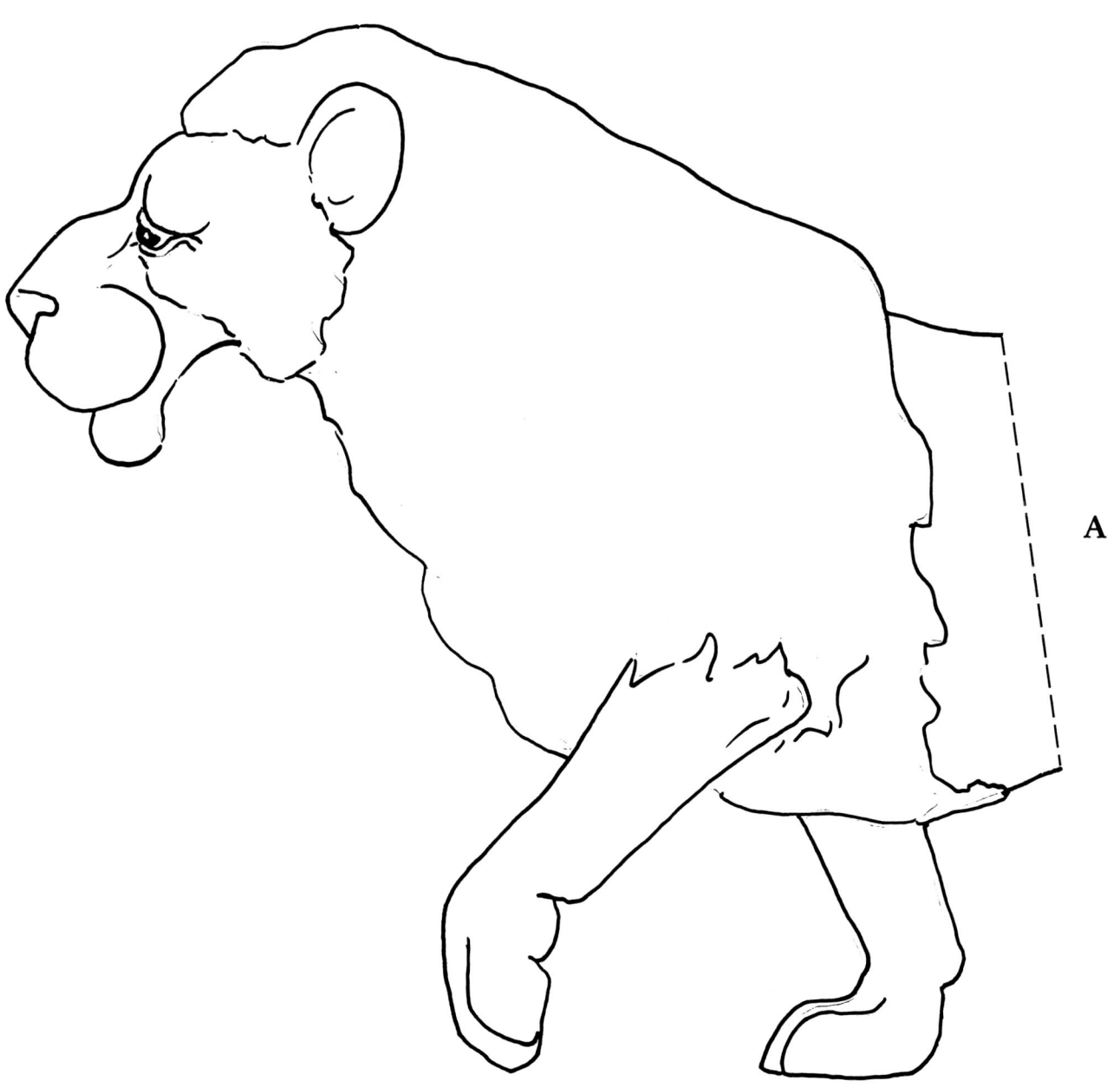

A

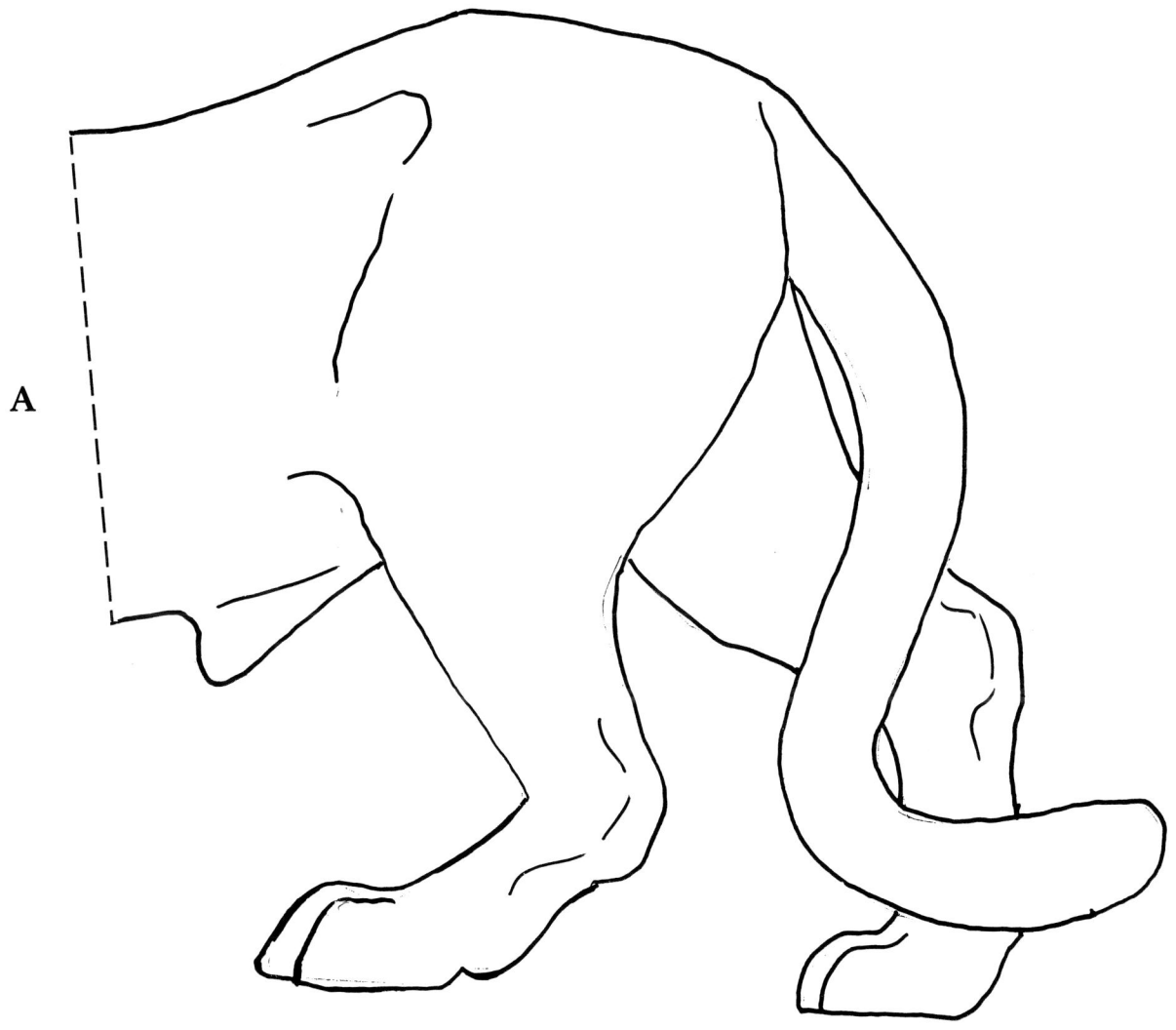

A

# Friendly Cougar

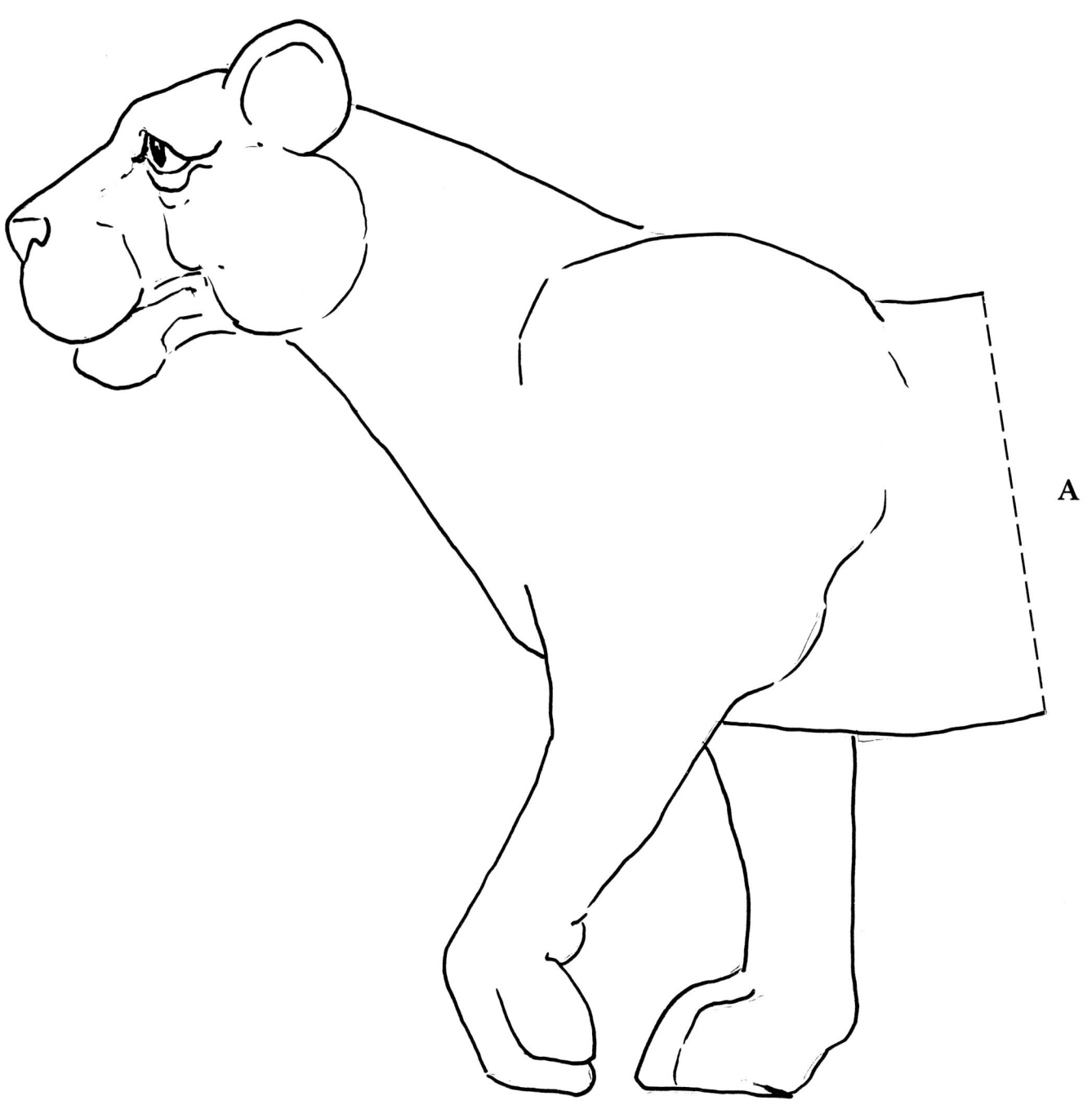

A

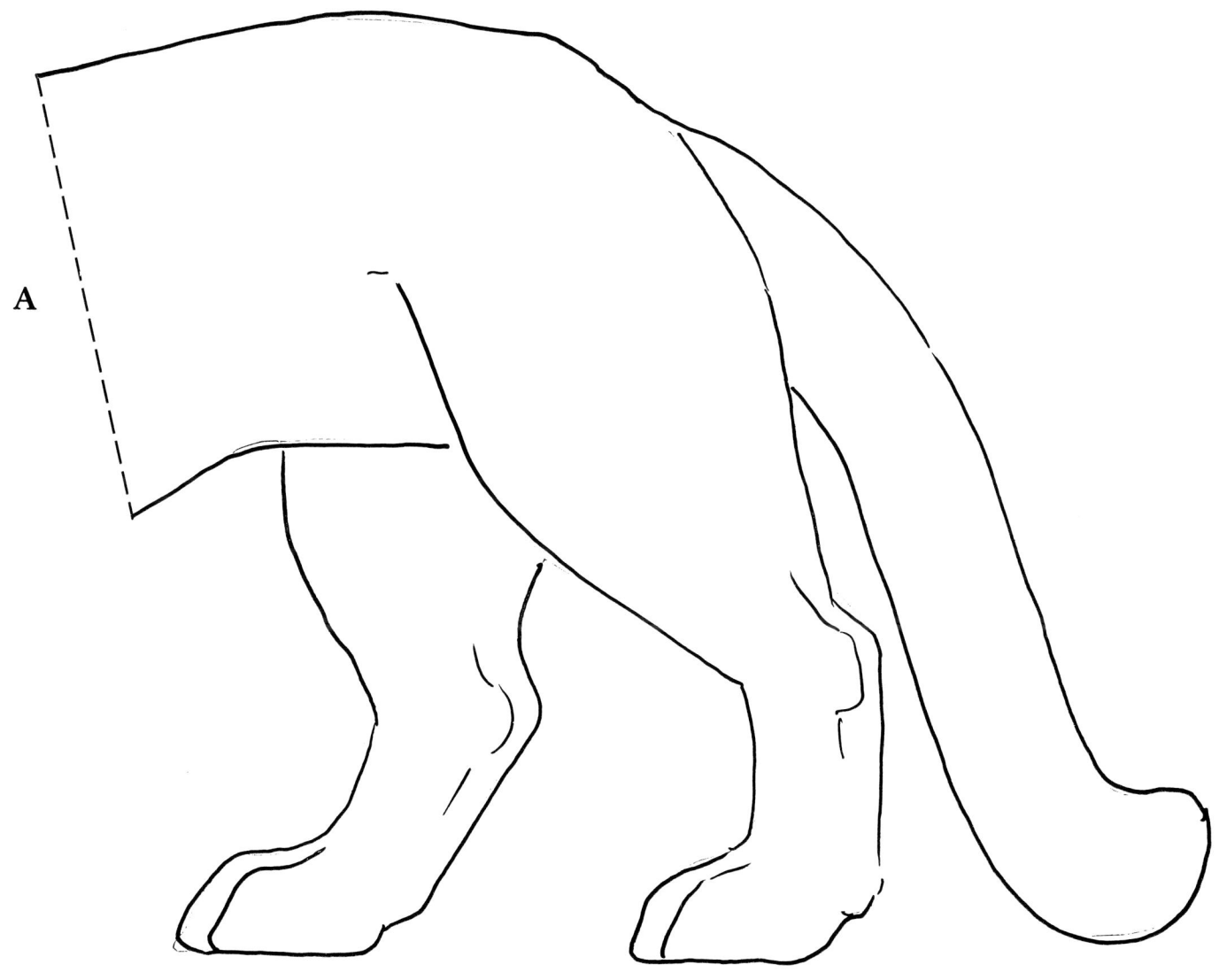

A

**Weasel**

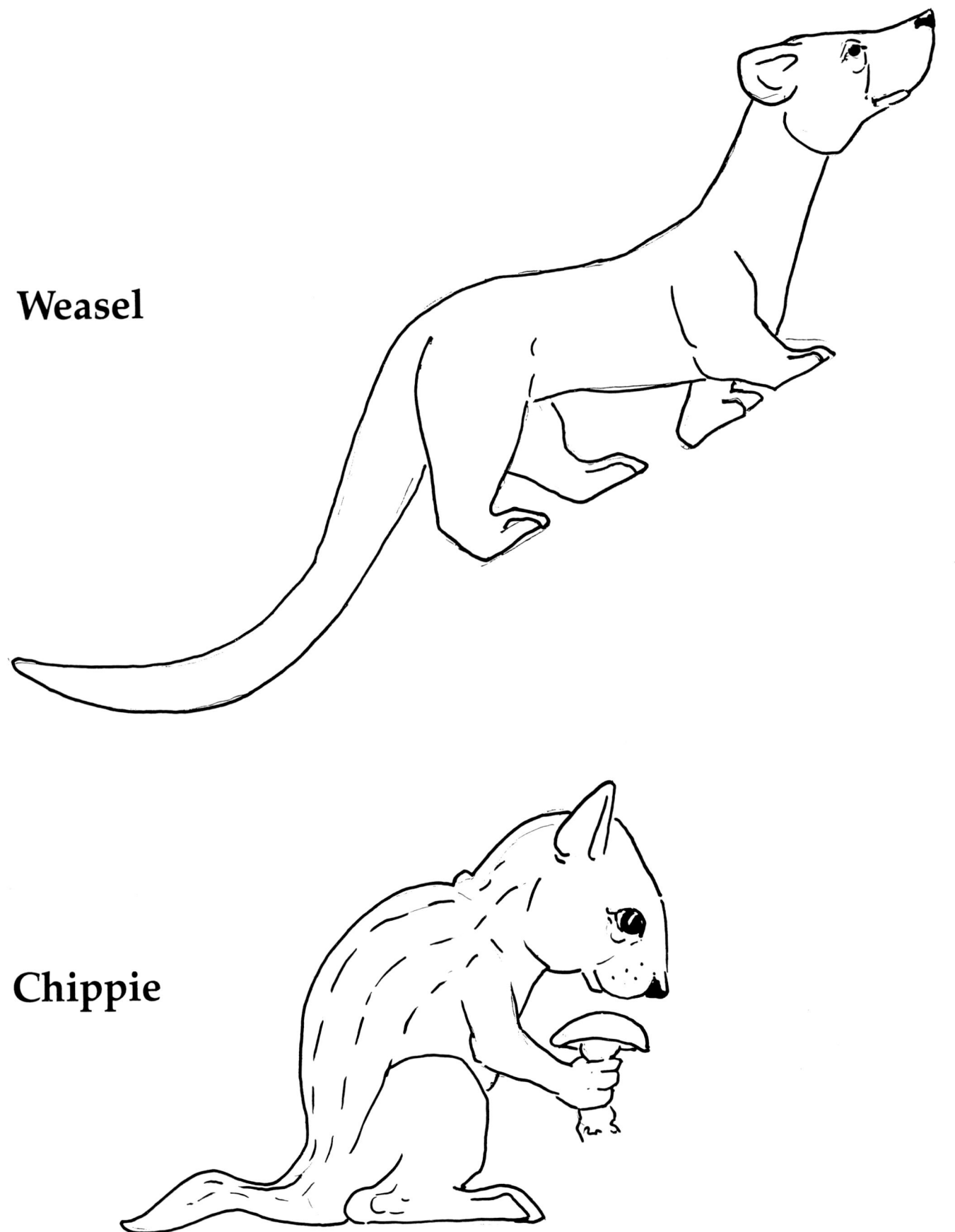

**Chippie**

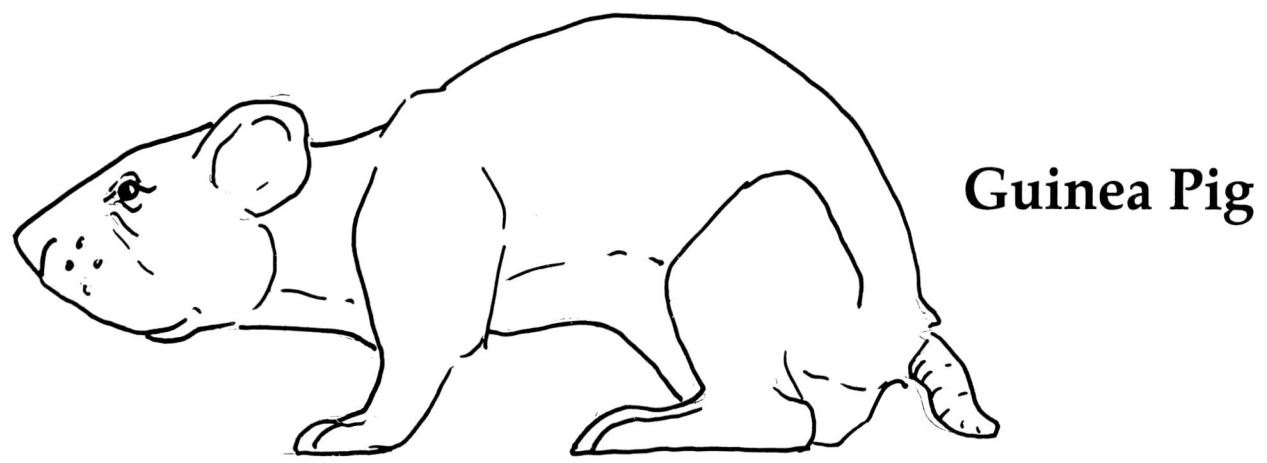

**Guinea Pig**

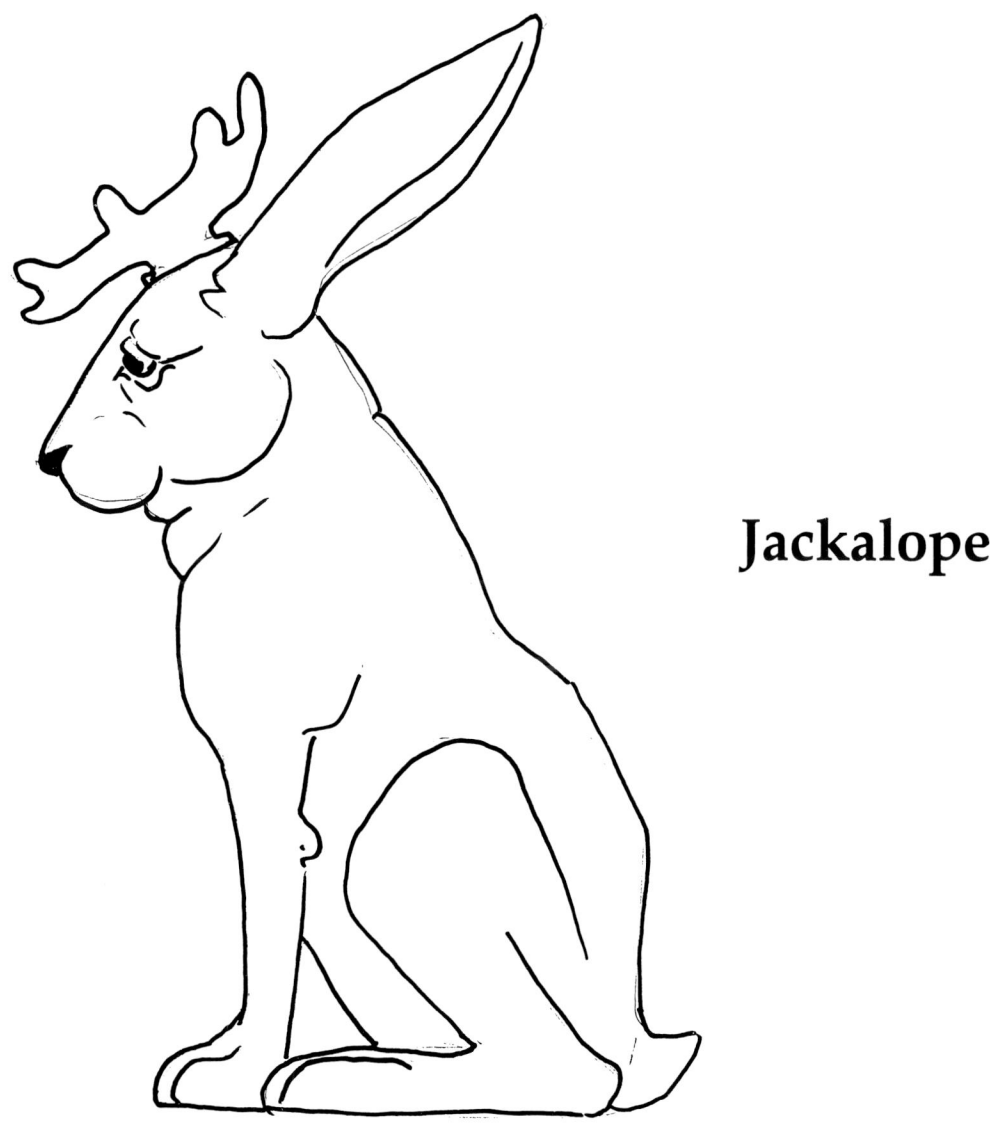

**Jackalope**

# Wolverine

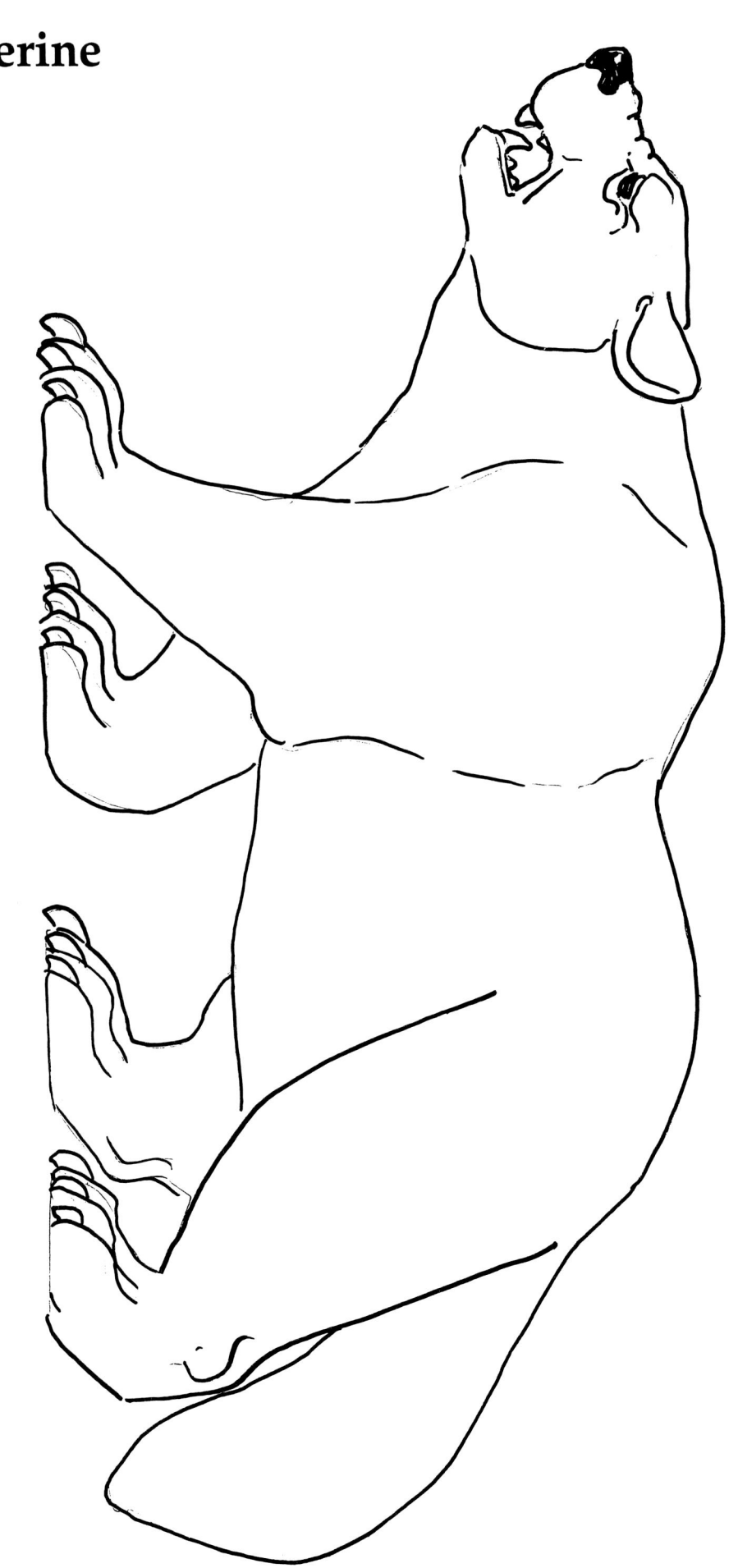

# Bruster Rooster

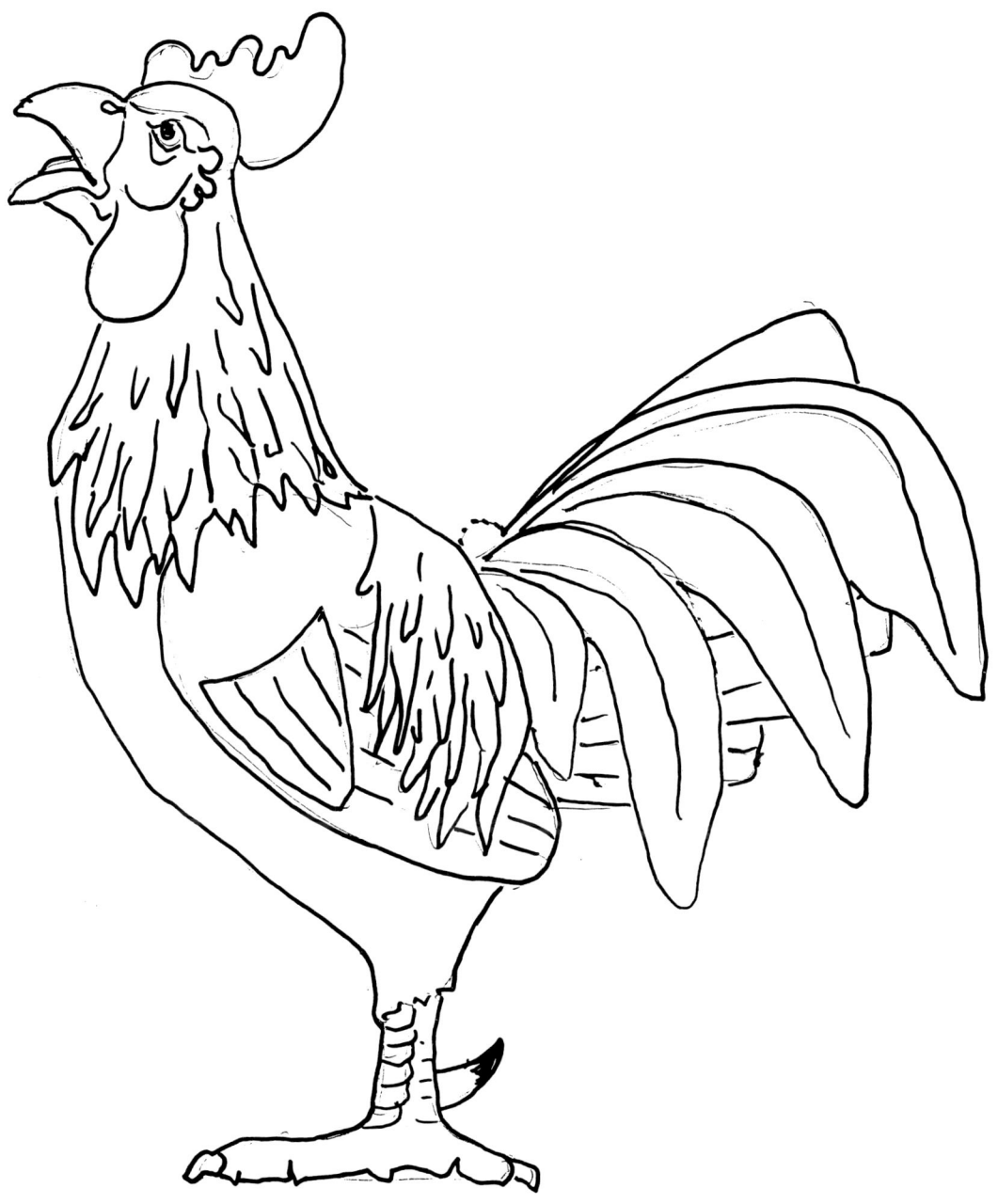

# Dragon Bust

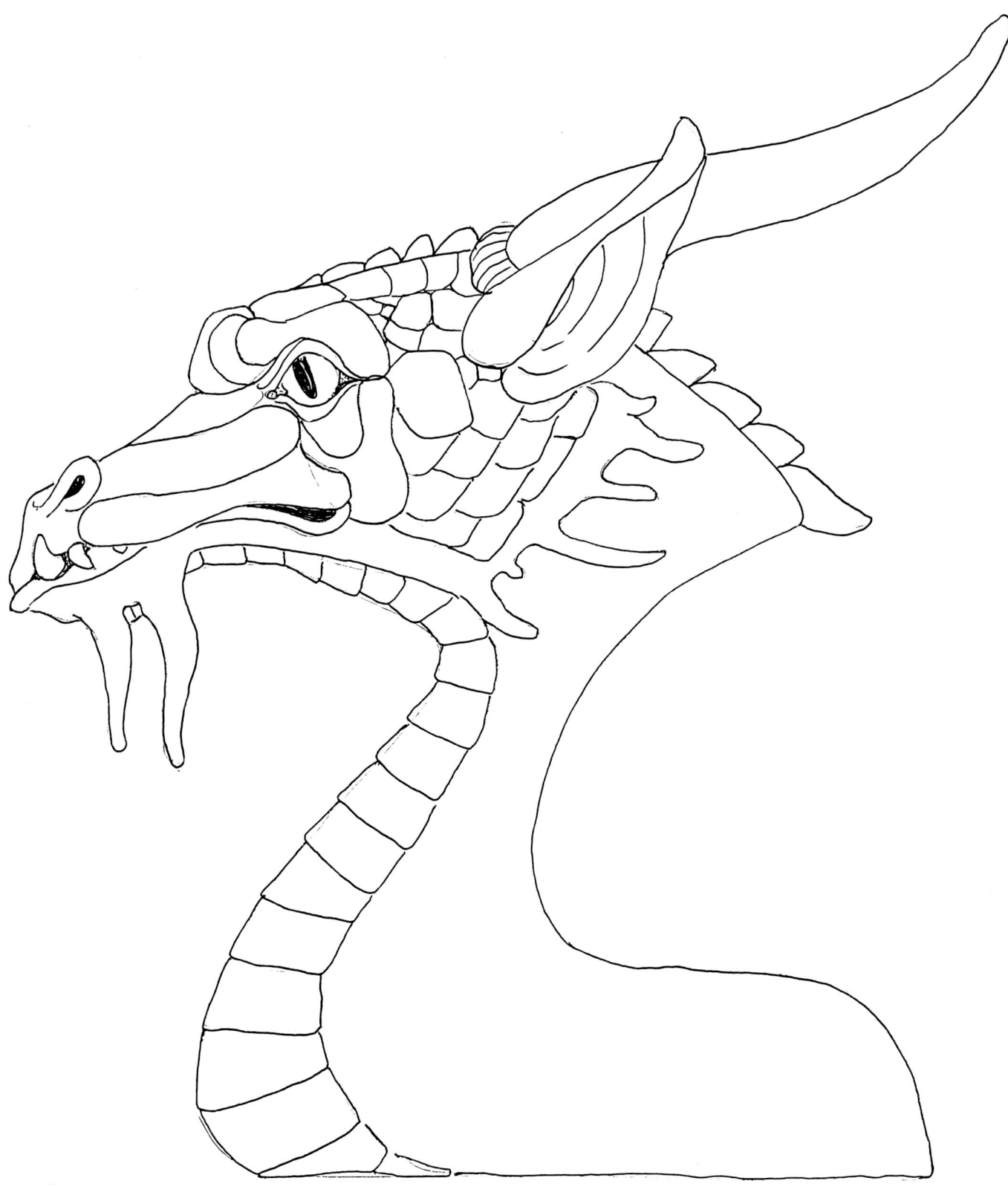